MORNING STAR'S
SEVEN STEPS TO

Spiritual
Awakening

A Book of Love in the Time of COVID-19

A Mindful Guide to Love, Life, and Unity During and After the Pandemic

REV. DR. JC HUSFELT

Print ISBN: 978-1-09833-636-3

eBook ISBN: 978-1-09833-637-0

Snowy Owl, Port Ludlow, WA

For my Family, Apprentices, the Earth, and Nature.

CONTENTS

Life is Struggle
We are in the time of the "Great Struggle."
Do not lose Heart
Keep Love and Hope alive in your Heart

We are tied together in the single garment of destiny, caught in an inescapable network of mutuality. And whatever affects one directly affects all indirectly.

— Dr. Martin Luther King, Jr.

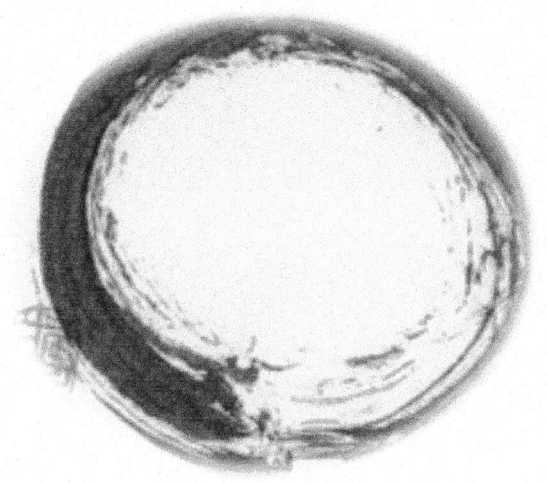

"Circle of vast space, lacking nothing and holding nothing in excess."[1]

This is Ensō: a universal symbol of wholeness and completion, the oneness of life, the spirit of harmonious cooperation, personal development and refinement of character, the unseen and seen.

Calligraphy by Dr. Husfelt

FOREWORD

I began writing this book, my sixth, before the onset of the pandemic. My goal was to assist people in spiritually awakening to love, magic, and life. A reflection of Sherry (Sher), my wife, and me of our love and power together. In its deepest meaning, love is unity—oneness. One 5 Star Review of our memoir, Tequila and Chocolate, stated: "a unique memoir that offers honest experiences, lessons that are spiritual and philosophical with the guiding message throughout being one of love, magic, and life."

Our 50th Wedding Anniversary, Tintagel, England 2017

The One, the All, the Creator is love. This divine universal love is the unity, the oneness, the glue of the universe, love which is all-embracing. Philosophically it is the mind and body of the One—the consciousness that connects all things in existence. It is the fullness of the moon reflected in a still pond on a star-studded night. The golden threads that weave a web between and through all living things with a song of divine love. For us, divine love is the unconditional actions that begin within us and extend out to all others. The greater our sense of oneness within ourselves and in others—the greater is our expression of divine universal love.

Our Seven Steps will help awaken this love within your heart—your inner *divine spark*. This is our book of love—our Seven Steps to Awakening. During this time of the "Great Struggle," keep love and hope alive within your heart—now and forever.

Rev. Dr. JC Husfelt

INTRODUCTION

*In the spiritual path both love and hope are necessary. If
you do not have these, you had better give up the quest.
We must learn to be patient. But is a lover ever patient? Be
patient and strong in the hope of finding someone who
will show you the way.*

—FERID UD DIN ATTAR[2] (THE CONFERENCE OF THE BIRDS)

In the Present and Future, More important than Ever—Love and Hope are needed... Now.

In October 2019, I led a small group of men to the Yucatan. A sacred land where I had first set foot during the Harmonic Convergence in August 1987. Over the years, Sher and I returned many times to this pristine, beautiful piece of paradise. The last time we were there was in 2005. Disheartened each time we returned by the destruction of this sacred land for development, all for money and greed, 2019 was even worse.

We spent our last three days in a small funky hotel overlooking an amazing white sand beach framing the beauty of the Caribbean Sea. My room was on the top floor of a three story cabaña with a thatched roof. At least in this part of the Yucatan, I was in heaven—sun, sand, and sky all enfolding a peaceful layer of tranquility. And then... the second night I was awoken by the sound of claws on the bed's wooden headboard. Startled awake, I turned on my flashlight. And there staring at me was—a bat with a broken wing!

I've always had a close relationship with bats. Such as three days before my vision on the Big Island of Hawaii in 1993. As I relate in our memoirs:

Early in the afternoon in bright sunlight, a bat flew towards me, my Hawaiian healer friend, and our son, Jamie. It circled around us once then disappeared. An omen my friend called it as the rest of our journey was magical and life-changing.

This was just one of my many unusual experiences with bats, many foretelling the future. This time the bat was injured and couldn't fly. Focusing my mind and eyes on the bat, I verbally explained that this was my sleeping place, and he/she needed to go outside on the terrace. With some give and take, and a little help, my "friend" went outside. I went back to a deep sleep.

The next morning, I looked everywhere on the terrace… no bat. The bat had disappeared! Later that day I saw the Innkeeper and shared my bat experience. "Impossible," was his reply. "There haven't been any bats around for a long time, and it couldn't have gotten-in through the thatched roof of your room."

I let his remarks linger in the air. No use trying to convince him that yes, I was in my seventies, but no, not delusional. After this encounter with the Innkeeper, I began wondered about the meaning of my visitor in the night. There was my connection with Anselmo Perez, a *Zinacantec* shaman from the mountainous city of San Juan Chamula. Outside of the highlands, few know about this "bat shaman" of Chamula. Zinacantec literally means "land of bats."[3] But what else was this wounded bat trying to tell me?

The entrance to San Juan Chamula's famous church, the *Iglesia de San Juan Bautista*, and the locals' rather untraditional use of it. There are no pews and it is dark and thick with incense, lit only by candles. No dogmatic preaching, no priest: worshipers simply sit on the floor with lines of candles around them or in front of them while praying.

Being in a familiar place, land of the Maya, I decided that when I returned home, I would research their connection to bats. I knew across the board that one of the outstanding characteristics of bats is their apparent ability to "see" in complete darkness. Once back in Washington State, my research revealed that to the Maya, the bat was much more than being able to see in the dark.

The bat was an emblematic symbol representing some group/groups—possibly humanity. Another role played by the bat is as a messenger, often paired on vessels with a bird. For the Maya, bats were, in fact, the nocturnal counterparts of hummingbirds. Furthermore, there is a direct link between bats and the Earth—explicit in bat iconography. The role of the bat as messenger and its association with Earth (caves) specifically pointed to a connection with Maya scribes. Since scribes are associated with caves, this clearly recognizes the role of the bat as a messenger from the gods to scribes.[4] *Ah tz'ib* (also spelled *ah ts'ib*) — a translation of this is "he who writes or paints." It is one of the terms the ancient Maya used for scribes.[5] I am a writer and calligrapher. To a certain degree, am I not a scribe? Interesting; by the way of a broken-winged bat, what were the gods trying to tell me?

* * *

And then… the bat-born message became loud and clear as the coronavirus raised its ugly head.[6] In a brief moment of time, life took on new meaning for all of us. We have all struggled at various times in our life. But now, we may be facing our greatest struggle in a lifetime—the "Great Struggle." We must keep love in our hearts, be in the present moment and the present day. Please do not let fear thrust you into the future. Stay in the present. Have discipline and perseverance until we come out the other side of this scourge.

In my other books, I have explored the transition from the Age of Pisces to the Age of Aquarius. With this pandemic we have now entered the birthing time, transitional time—the "Great Struggle," before the beginning of the Aquarian Age. With any birth, there is "pain" before the actual birth. I knew there needed to be a "shock" to business as usual, to the inequalities, discrimination, racism, and sexism of society, capitalism, and organized religion. Some extraordinary event and/or happenings, a birthing time, which would enable us to make the leap to the Aquarian Age. Possibly a world war and/or earth changes due to climate change but not a pandemic, even though this novel coronavirus will definitely be earth changing. To my dismay… there still might be war, possibly a civil war.

* * *

Aquarius is the foretold Golden Age, of wholeness or Oneness. An Age of the heart, truth, freedom, equality, and of course, love. This Age of Gold is a time of the Unicorn and the Feathered Serpent. A time to uncover our own "horn of light" (pineal gland) and our blending of heaven (feathered) and earth (serpent).

The Mesoamericans call the Golden Age, the Sixth Sun. It is to be *Xochitl Tonatiuh* explained poetically as the Sun of Flowers—when humanity comes to flower. This is Jesus' Sun and Quetzalcóatl's Sun, the Sun of Consciousness. It will be the Age of the Divine Human – *Hombre-Dios*. The deity symbolizing the Sixth Sun is "*Xochiquétzal*, goddess of flowers. As the 'House of Flowers,' the human heart, we understand that *xóchitl* here symbolizes the budding blossom of the human spirit at last freed from duality."[7] The Sixth Sun – a time to look forward to as *xóchitl* is love and the search for union. It is happiness. It is sex.

Another manner in which to view the Sixth Sun is to listen to a Hopi Native American elder describing a Golden Age long forgotten: "We were created equal of oneness, living in a spiritual way, where life is everlasting. We were happy and at peace with our fellow men. All things were plentiful, provided by our Mother Earth upon which we were placed."[8]

* * *

The pandemic has caused most people to re-examine their lives and has shown us how we are interdependent on each other. This invisible enemy has revealed and shined a light on "normal." A normal that was broken and killing us through lack of health care for all, and the economics where over half of us were living paycheck to paycheck with little or no savings.

Our entire culture suffers from severe doses of induced conformity imposed by schools, churches, television commercials, and peer pressure requiring adherence to the latest, academically accepted ideas and commercial fads. Contemporary cultures seek to breed conformity to social, cultural, moral, and economic values bred by that culture as a means of perpetuating the system in place and the class of people entrusted with governing that system. The consequence is witnessed in contemporary cultures' ties to economic models in which the only acceptable values can be reduced to money and income: the amassing of wealth, proving the individual's relative power within the culture through the amount and quantity of expenditures as witnessed in the things one acquires, and dedication to productive work which is really only guaranteed to amass greater sums for the already wealthy while reducing the free time and enjoyment of the worker classes. All of these modes of economically induced conformity engage with sense perception in a way as to create a cycle of reinforcement. Consequently, the mind is more and more attached to sense perceived reality as being all there is—a reality that is only dualistic. And therein lies the dysfunction and problem with our culture and society.[9]

* * *

The world and us all ebb and flow through cycles of change. It is inevitable, and the only thing that is predictable. Step out of your present situation for a moment and ask yourself, what can I become? How does my life journey progress from this point forward? Yes, it is a struggle, but all of us can do it together.

In every crisis, lies great opportunity. This is our opportunity to build a better future. To think is to create. We need to think about what we wish to create. We need to set a goal and take small, disciplined steps in order to achieve it—this is our Seven Steps.

The past is crumbling so that we can revolutionize and rebuild something new. The familiarity of the past can be our guide, but the hope and the promise of the future can guide us to think bigger and better. There are chances here to upgrade and change our lives.

Time is now, and right for personal, cultural, social, economic, political, and religious transformation—death of the old, rebirth of the new. A revolutionary tomorrow is possible. This "revolutionary new" is an egalitarian culture and way of life filled with love, compassion, and kindness. And a Green Philosophy where we respect and are in partnership with all things of the earth. This is the opportunity to stop, possibly reverse, destructive climate change. We are all a "work in progress." Let us work together. We need unity and the most important point is to make this unity last. This book will help us take that first step and begin to achieve this and unite us as One in love and power as all of us and the planet "blossom" together.

Home

There are silver linings resulting from the pandemic. One focuses on home as "millions of Americans are taking part in an unprecedented experiment in working from home. Many are happier, more efficient and want to hang onto the benefits when the pandemic ends... Many people who had never considered this kind of working life have now had a taste of it, and they love it."[10]

Power... and what is the greatest power... Love. Our home is a sanctuary of love, the power and love of family—unity. Home is our soul. Home does not mean house. And for the ones with multiple houses, they are not a home. Wealth does not equal home. Heart and love equal home.

A sense of place is the product of lived space and lived time, a reflection of our states of heart and mind. Home is where the heart is. Home is important for sense of self. This is one of the reasons why homelessness is such a blight and stain on our culture considering the amount of wealth of the elites. Keep in mind, when wealth is hoarded, the person has a heart that is extremely dull/dark/heavy—the person is flawed within—no amount of church going, or so-called philanthropy will solve it.

For the majority of people, the amount of time at work in the past has eclipsed time spent at home with family all together. Basically, as wage-slaves, many work for survival but for others, the excessive consumption of things. Home has turned into a house, a place to sleep not a place of loving togetherness, what the Hawaiians call *Ohana*. This concept is based on a sense of unity, mutual interdependence, mutual help, emotional support given and received, and most importantly, love.

During and after this pandemic consider adapting as much as possible the Hawaiian concept of *Ohana,* including the *aloha* (love, compassion) spirit. *Ohana* was based on the values of *aloha* - love, *ho'okipa* - hospitality, *ho'oponopono* - setting right/forgiveness, and *tokahi* - unity. *Ohana* means the spirit of "oneness and the love that is the breath of the soul. It is a loving state of mind where hate has no resting place. To the Hawaiian's *aloha* represents love. All of life was founded on this love, the love of the sea, the love of the sky and the love of the *'aina* (land), and all its inhabitants. And to these beautiful people, the greatest earthly expression of this love was the love of family, the *ohana*.

"*Ohana* is not like the Western concept of family, which is becoming more fractured as time passes. The *ohana* refers to an extended family ideal, which includes not only the immediate family of mother, father, children, and grandparents but also all things of the land, the sea, and the sky as well as the *'aum kua* (a family god, often a deified ancestor). In the spirit of *aloha*, all things of the *ohana* are respected and cared for in a loving and meaningful way. An integral member of the *ohana* is the kupuna (elder) who is regarded as the keeper of knowledge and wisdom."[11]

Another culture we may turn to for knowledge on the importance and power of home is the ancient Greeks and their goddess of the hearth—*Hestia*. "Few myths, statues, or temples remain of *Hestia;*

she is rarely personified, yet before life became focused away from the home, she was the most honored goddess, worshipped at the center of every household.

"As the hearth, *Hestia* is the center and focus of the home, the curator of family life, offering a place where our circle of ancestors can gather. As custodian of the hearth, she personifies the fire burning at the heart of life, the fireplace of the home, and the flame lit in the city center. She is the Olympic flame that will burn even though the games cannot be played. She sustains the inner world but has been forgotten in the stampede of outer life. Formerly consigned to the unconscious, she has reappeared in the center of this pandemic."[12]

* * *

Maintaining a state of wellness is essential. Stay safe, and keep others safe, by cooking and sharing meals together at home. At the very least it's important to eat as simply and cleanly as you can. Fresh fruits and vegetables, whole grains, nuts, legumes, low fat dairy or nut milks and if non-vegetarian, fresh fish and poultry with occasional beef. Buy organic and grass fed options as often as you can as they are free of pesticides and chemicals and hormone disruptors which adversely affect the immune system which will lower the body's ability to fight off infections and potential diseases or chronic illnesses. Many grocers are now stocking healthier food choices with more reasonable prices making it more economically possible to eat food that is more sustainable and better for our wellbeing.

Play music, make music, and dance. Exercise at home. Consider doing the following: Begin laying on the floor, slowly close your eyes and still your mind while deep breathing from the "tummy," maintain slow breathing; next stretching while on your back and then standing stretching, open the door and walk or run outside (masking if necessary), come back home, and complete with sit-ups, push-ups, stretching once again, and finish with meditation. This is a very brief and simple example of an exercise series.

Consistency is the key to health and power. Eat properly and exercise at least three to four times a week working up to five or six. But always rest at least once or twice a week. Rest is important. And attempt to quiet the "chatter" in your mind at night and sleep like a "baby" seven to eight hours each night. Motivation to be healthy (such as proper nutrition), exercise, spiritual, and mental "health/exercise" needs to come from within yourself—just do it.

Most importantly consider spending at least 15 minutes a day connecting with people close to you. This will help you feel less alone. One of our basic teachings is "listen, look, and learn." When listening to others give your undivided attention. Listen not only with your ears but with your heart. Listen to the sound of the person's voice, the vibration/quality, the silence, and what was not said, but can be sensed.

Another method to maintain a state of wellness is by conducting a *Moai*, a Japanese term for a social support group. This small group could even be just two friends who convene by phone, video chat, or in person maintaining social-distancing and share their true feelings about personal issues related to health, relationships, and other manners pressing on their mind.

Our daughter Jess, me, Sher, and our son Jamie during my 60th birthday celebration in 2006 in Delphi, Greece

During and after this pandemic, practice a new togetherness. With the setting sun, all work would be finished. Spend time remembering days of old, tell stories, sing/dance, make music, play games, and so forth. It is a time for joy, a time for love, and a time for family. It is a time when memories and togetherness are precious and eternal. And one final thought. Transform your home into a "place of Awakening" — a place of Love.

Awakening

The owl is the secret symbol for the guardian of the invisible world.
To those who have understood that Love is the
key, the White Owl[13] will appear, and will lead them
into another time. One cycle ends, but another
commences - and a seed group will go forward into
the Age of Aquarius, the Age of the Holy Spirit.[14]

One word. The key to awakening our hearts and minds, one word—Love. Love means oneness, the glue that binds the universe together. In our journey of awakening to love, we need to explore the mysteries of life. Many times, throughout the twists and turns of our existence, we have wondered about the following universal questions: What is death and what is the meaning of life? Who are we, where are we going? Is there such a thing as reincarnation? Is life truly everlasting? What is God? These are just a few of the divine mysteries that are a part of the great Mystery. These mysteries are to be sought after - and in the seeking you will experience - and in the experience you will understand - and in the understanding you will know - and this knowing will be based on your own knowledge and wisdom.

Who am I? This is one of the most basic questions of life. Pondering and discovering the answer to this question will help us understand our purpose in life and will result in a life lived in love not in fear. If we do not know who we truly are and our purpose in life, our world feels foreign and takes on a picture encased frame filled with hues of fear and stress.

The only problem facing you in life is
Your belief in separation from the Source.
Solve that one and all the others will vanish.[15]

The knowledge presented in this book, and my other five books,[16] will revolutionize our thinking about ourselves, others and nature so that we will come to see the common thread which binds us all together, and we will perceive the enormous potential we have for awakening and the creation of a new humanity. We are standing on the threshold of a new consciousness of radical nonduality, bubbling under the surface, its energies waiting to be united and unleashed. Together we can achieve this.[17] We can get through this pandemic.

* * *

My knowledge has been accumulated from my experience of "listening, looking and learning" from indigenous elders, healers, and shamans from all over the world. It also comes from my interactions with the young and old of other races and cultures and emanates deeply from my own soul wisdom. This knowledge is what I refer to as the "first knowledge"—first principles. It is knowledge that is woven throughout and found in all the "first people" indigenous spiritual/religious traditions on this earth.

I am a philosopher, which means my mission is to establish the relation of manifested things to their invisible ultimate cause or nature. Plato regarded philosophy as the greatest good ever imparted by Divinity to humans. Philosophy has been defined as: the science of things divine and human, and the causes in which they are contained

[Cicero]; the science of things evidently deduced from first principles [Descartes].[18]

The One Who Plants Trees Knowing That He Will Never Sit in Their
Shade, Has At Least Started to Understand the Meaning of Life.
—Rabindranath Tagore

Awakening is centered on one fundamental principle: each of us is divine and carries a spark, a micro-star, a micro-sun within our hearts and DNA. This divine spark/fire is the essence and foundational pearl of our life. Humans are not the only ones that contain a spark of divinity within. Everything has this spark—trees, animals, stars, and even black holes. In addition, everything has an intrinsic identity and value. Therefore, trees are not only divine, but are also intrinsically unique as they provide such things as shelter and food. This concept is part of the foundational bases of the spiritual philosophy/personal religion of Divine Humanity.

The Seven Steps are not a quick fix or instant awakening. It takes commitment, focus, persistence, support, perseverance, and struggle. Yes, there is struggle - the "Great Struggle," and most assuredly, suffering and sacrifice to get to the other side of this novel coronavirus. At the same time, we need to face and release fear of the unknown and come to terms with the dysfunction darkness within us, and the unresolved woundings' of our past. This takes courage and resolve. Keep love and hope in your heart. During this most difficult time, our faith is that your spirit will be uplifted, inspired, and brightened by your journey through our Seven Steps.

THE SEVEN STEPS

1. Know Thyself

2. Accept the Power Within

3. Accept a Green Philosophy: Experience and Embrace the Magic of Mother Nature

4. Experience the Moment-to-Moment Love and Magic of Life

5. Be Gentle but Firm

6. Nothing in Excess

7. Keep the Measure

OUR FOUNDATIONAL PEARL - DIVINE HUMANITY

The mother sea and fountainhead of all religions lie in the mystical experiences of the individual. All theologies, all ecclesiasticisms are secondary growths, superimposed.

– WILLIAM JAMES

We are all in this together. Like all transitional times, ours is fraught with perils and possibilities. The pandemic has revealed the scale of the dysfunctional "normal" that people have accepted. This normal was based on greed, inequity, extraction, and sexism to name just a few of them. This accepted normal has included environmental destruction, poverty and homelessness, a blind eye to climate change, gender inequality, racial and gay discrimination, lack of health care affordability and availability, and on and on. The worst thing would be a return to this normal.

The established paradigms on this earth are corrupt and broken. These patriarchal economic, governmental, and religious systems have based their existence on spreading fear and separatism while accumulating excessive amounts of wealth and power for their controlling elite at the expense of the rest of humanity and the earth.[19]

It is no consequence that being on the cusp of a Golden age, we experience a pandemic and then the overwhelming rage and subsequent demonstrates throughout the U.S. surrounding the murder of an African-American, George Floyd.

Down throughout history, pandemics and social unrest have forced people to break with the past and establish new paradigms and beliefs. This one is no different and provides a gateway to transition from the Age of Pisces to the Age of Aquarius. Instead of going back to the old normal, the old paradigms, we need something new such as an awakened egalitarian society, a civilization spread throughout the width and breath of our beautiful planet—one of peace, kindness, love, forgiveness, equality, and oneness. Anchoring this awakened society would be the living philosophical paradigm of Divine Humanity.

A Spiritual Philosophy and Wisdom Religion

Divine Humanity ("Humanity" represents not only the human race but all things of creation) is a living spiritual philosophy and new consciousness. It is also a pure religion of the people, by the people and for all the people. Divine Humanity is a Religion of Philosophy and a living personal (not institutionalized) religion. As a world philosophy of awe and a religion of equality and simplicity, it conveys a love for all forms of life and acknowledges everything in creation as divine as well as honoring its own unique intrinsic expression. Therefore, not only is every human being a divine human with an intrinsic human expression and the light, holy spark, of God (the ONE, the Great Mystery) within them, but all trees have the divine spark within them and in their intrinsic expression may provide food and shelter for us and for other creatures of the earth. In other words, the ONE exists in ALL and the ALL exists in ONE.

Divine Humanity is a personal religion and spiritual philosophy that is based on one's truth found within one's heart and mind. It is not based on faith, dogma, or doctrine. It is a green,[20] ecological and egalitarian philosophy and religion. Divine Humanity recognizes the divine in nature and the sacredness of all living things. "Nature in partnership" is one of the hallmarks of Divine Humanity. It acknowledges the equality and divinity of nature and the realization that humanity is not above nature, as a steward; nor below nature, at the mercy of it;

but is one with nature and in partnership with the earth in co-creating a paradisiacal state of life, for all life.

Since each of us has the spark, the starlight of God, within us, **Divine Humanity believes that we are born in original divinity,**[21] **not original sin.**[22] We are "born in *love* and not in sin. There is no love greater or holier than that of mother and child. There is nothing more sinless—baptized or not—than the child in the mother's arms. Woe unto him who dare offend one of these little ones, *for of such is the kingdom of heaven.*"[23]

Of course, the Church sees it differently. Thomas Aquinas, a 13th Century Italian Dominican friar, Catholic priest, and Doctor of the Church, "believed that the original sin of Eve was repeated every time anyone made love, married or otherwise. It would appear that Christianity is the only religion in the history of our planet in which it is sinful just to be alive."[24]

* * *

Divine Humanity is based on the concept of non-differentiating knowledge. This is the knowledge that fuses into non-duality all dichotomies such as subject and object. In other words, Divine Humanity is not based on dualism.[25]

Since there is no separation; no dualism—just two aspects of a single reality. We may be enlightened and deluded, even defiled, and pure at the same time. An example of this is discovered within the biblical myth of Samson—the honey (pure) within the carcass of the lion, or beast (defiled). And of course, we have the lotus that lives in mud (defiled) but opens its beauty (purity) as the light of the sun awakens it.

The Divine Spark[26] - *Scintilla*

Divine Humanity believes that every person has a divine fire within them—a seed of divine light: The Divine Immanence. This is the spark of uncreated fire of the Absolute, the universal seed of all beings. This seed of divine light may be likened to a mustard seed within our hearts. This divine seed of immortality or spark, which sometimes may be referred to as the *divine golden dew*[27], constitutes the Soul — an eternal spark in its essence, since it is a fragment of God, and immortal.[28]

This is our sacred self. This inner seed of light, that settles over and interpenetrates our DNA as *divine golden dew*, needs to be awakened, to grow in its brilliance and to be brought to the surface and nourished until its radiance suffuses the world.[29] This is our luminous body that grows within and shines without. In so doing, our relationship to ourselves and to all other things of the world is transformed from being based on fear to being based on love.

Each one of us has a heavenly lineage—a heavenly DNA (based on previous lives) and an earthly lineage—parental DNA. Our soul is the totality of our incarnations blended with our divine fire (spark). Our divine golden dew is our **intrinsic** Divine or Golden Proportion. At birth, our intrinsic Golden Proportion flows over and blends with our intrinsic earthly DNA. We are Divine, we are Human.

Scintilla

Scintilla is a minute particle; a tiny trace; a tiny spark; in our case, our inner divine spark. In the past our divine spark has been esoterically called the Blue Stone or the Blue Apple—Blue (divine particle/spark) Apple (knowledge, immortality). In other words, the hidden meaning of Blue Apples concerns the knowledge that we each have a divine spark (immortality) within us. This was the original knowledge and message of Jesus and Mary Magdalene—the kingdom within us and the kingdom outside us in nature, the earth, and the heavens.

We might ask, why the color blue? It refers to the color of a flame. The inner core of the candle flame is light blue, with a temperature of around 1800 K (1500 °C). That is the hottest part of the flame.

Above us, stars have differing intensities of heat and that heat is related to color. The hottest star is the blue star. There is a Hopi prophecy concerning the Blue Star, which signals the return of *Pahana* or "True White Brother." "As above, so below," the blue star reflects the starlight within us

And then we have the magic of light-emitting diodes, which are unique in producing white light. This is due to the fact that the electric current (negative and positive) itself is the light, unlike incandescent bulbs or fluorescent lights.

The birth of light-emitting diodes only came after the creation of blue diodes. Up until that time, the only diodes available were red and green, and without a blue diode, white light cannot be created. When red, green, and blue diodes are combined and "an electric field is applied, negative and positive charges meet in the middle layer and combine to produce photons of light."[30] In other words, with the blending or interpenetration of negative and positive or, if you will, symbolic spirit and matter – heaven and earth, light is produced, i.e. luminous body.

> *And that stone is both pure and precious*
> *Its name hast thou never heard*
> *Men call it "lapis exilis"*[31]
> *By its magic the wonderous bird*
> *The phoenix becomes ashes*
> *And yet does such virtue flow from the stone*
> *That afresh it riseth*
> *Renewed from the ashes grown.*[32]

The most famous mystery concerning Blue Stones or Blue Apples is connected with Rennes-le-Château, France, made famous by the publication of *The Da Vinci Code* in May of 2002. We are remarkably familiar with Rennes-le-Château, located within the rugged wine country of Languedoc region of Southern France, having first traveled there in November of 1998. Surrounded by a mystical aura while tucked away in the shadows of the snow-capped peaks of the Pyrenees, Rennes trusts you into an alternative reality. Add to this, the numerous tales of hidden fabulous treasure.

The mysteries and legends connected with Rennes-le-Château not only points to treasure but also relates to the Holy Grail and the theories surrounding Jesus and Mary Magdalene. One of these theories concerns the marriage between Jesus and Mary, which was initially made popular by the book *Holy Blood, Holy Grail* released in 1982. Another mystery was the meaning of *A Midi Pommes Bleues*— "at Midday Blue Apples." These mysteries intrigued illustrious men of genius who traveled there such as Leonardo da Vinci, Isaac Newton, Jules Verne, Voltaire, Richard Wagner, and the 17th century painter Nicolas Poussin. As much as they searched, they never discovered the secret treasure of Rennes-le-Château: the secret of the Blue Apples.

Sher, Tour Magdala, Rennes-le-Château

Since 1988 we have journeyed to Rennes-le-Château many times, alone and sometimes leading a group. A few of our tales are documented in our memoirs: *Tequila and Chocolate, The Adventures of the Morning Star and Soulmate.* From our memoirs:

Since the release of The Da Vinci Code in May of 2002, more people are aware of the various mysteries that shroud Rennes-le-Château like a dreary mist in a good, old-fashioned Dracula movie. The main mystery has to do with treasure… if the priceless treasure is the hidden knowledge of Jesus's true message and teachings, would it be possible to prove this by using common sense, logical thinking, and intuition? The clues could possibly be found within a parchment, and most certainly in the many symbolic images scattered throughout the region. This knowledge of Jesus's true teachings and beliefs would be easier to discover than the physical evidence proving his survival of crucifixion. The decade-ago controversy surrounding The Da Vinci Code and a possible bloodline would pale in comparison to revealed truth about Jesus and his message. Yes, he was married to his special Mary of Bethany, but the "greatest lie ever told" is not about his marital status. The fact is, his being married or not does not really collapse the foundation of Christianity. The truth about Jesus and Mary's message does.

"I and the Father (Absolute) are One;
and the Truth will set you Free!."

Since I first set-foot on the hilltop sacred site of Rennes-le-Château, I have been pondering the meaning of its mysterious "Blue Apples." A friend, Elizabeth Van Buren, referred to Rennes-le-Château as "Refuge of the Apocalypse." Apocalypse (ἀποκάλυψις) is a Greek word meaning "revelation", "an unveiling or unfolding of things not previously known and which could not be known apart from the unveiling." Finally, after all this time, I was able to unveil and discover the meaning of *A Midi Pommes Bleues*— "at Midday Blue Apples."

To discover the truth, we must travel to the past during the time of the mysterious parish priest Berenger Saunière of Rennes-le-Château and its Tour Magdala: the Church of Mary Magdalene. One day in 1891 Saunière while making repairs on the badly decaying church altar discovered a cache of ancient parchments concealed in wooden tubes. One of the parchments could be called the Blue Apples parchment.

The Blue Apples Parchment begins with the word "Jesus." It tells the story of Jesus having dinner in Bethany with Lazarus and Mary Magdalene. It contains the most profound secret teachings of Jesus; the means to awaken to the land of Amor (Love - Oneness). The Blue Apples symbolize these secret teachings.

After the discovery of the parchments, Saunière did sometime that points us further to the meaning of Blue Apples. He did a renovation of the church dedicated to the Magdalene. One primary change. He installed stain-glass windows with one portraying Lazarus. It is from the stained-glass window of Lazarus that light shines through and creates the appearance of "blue apples" or "blue stones" on the church's wall at midday on July 22, the day honoring Mary Magdalene.

Why a Lazarus window and not one of Mary Magdalene? A further clue. The resurrection of Lazarus is typical of shamanic resurrection or rebirth done through water immersion or emergence from burial (symbolically in the earth or a cave).[33] This rebirth may result in awakening and the realization that the fire the divine spark (Blue Apples) of God or the Divine is within us, within our heart. This is when we realize that we are one with the nondual transcendent—our immanent radical nonduality, Oneness. This is our message and the true message of Jesus and Mary Magdalene—we all have within us, the divine spark—*scintilla*, symbolically a blue apple![34]

The whole universe seen and unseen, is the bread of life on which we live, and we are the crucible in which personality is forged.[35]

Our message of Divine Humanity states that the Otherworld (unseen universe) and this world (seen universe) interpenetrate as One—permeate each other. Since both interpenetrate, they must have a common structural element. This common element is Divine Mind/ Consciousness. Furthermore, all things have consciousness and are connected in a web of love. In other words, within the relative universe, the unseen and seen world mutually permeate each other. This theme of non-dual interpenetration underpins all aspects of Divine Humanity. This philosophy is substantiated by the work of the physicist David Bohm (1917 – 1992) a colleague of Albert Einstein.

Furthermore, Divine Humanity (wherein humanity represents not only the human race but all things of creation) is a living spiritual philosophy, a green religion – organic and natural. It calls for a new consciousness. Divine Humanity, a personal religion of spiritual philosophy, is based on one's truth found within one's heart. It is not based on faith, dogma, or doctrine.

Professor Huston Smith believes down to the soles of his feet that there is a true religion under all religions and that it is grounded in a mystical theism.

Divine Humanity is a mystical theism, a religious philosophy, and a living, personal—not institutionalized—religion. It is a religion and philosophy of heaven and Earth. The patriarchal western religions of Judaism, Christianity, and Islam are strictly heaven-patriarchal-based monotheistic (god) religions while the polytheistic (goddess) religions of the past were Earth based. Divine Humanity is based on both: the experience, knowledge, and wisdom of heaven and Earth. It is a radical nondualistic religion and philosophy and does not espouse belief in an anthropomorphic god[36] including the concept of grace. Additionally, Divine Humanity is not faith-based but grounded in common sense, truth of one's heart, and the reality of the equality, consciousness, and the interconnection of all things. In other words, we do not believe in the Divine (God); we know the Divine through direct experience.

As a world philosophy of awe and a religion of equality (neither patriarchal nor matriarchal) and simplicity, it conveys a love for all forms of life and acknowledges everything in creation as divine, as well as honoring its own unique intrinsic expression. Every human being is divine with an intrinsic human expression and the light, holy spark, of the reflection of the Absolute within—the spark of uncreated fire, universal seed of all beings. The Absolute is the transcendent great mystery outside of space and time, or God if you wish. In other words, within the relative universe (unseen world and seen world) all things are immanent; all have this light, this sacred fire of the One's uncreated fire within them and outside them. All things are divine and have a unique intrinsic expression. Trees, for example, have this sacred fire within them and in their intrinsic expression may provide food and shelter for us and for other creatures of the Earth. Therefore, the Great Mystery, the One, the Absolute (God) is both transcendent and immanent.

We do not need to be saved but to discover the oneness of being.

Divine Humanity synthesizes the religious and the philosophical. It is a philosophy of whole systems based on the premise that there is an underlying unity behind the nature of things. Its foundation and worldview are interpenetrating radical nonduality – oneness.[37] This is unity through duality, a unity created when the dualities of spirit and matter interpenetrate as one.

Moreover, it is a philosophical religion of peace and respect, and teaches you how-to live in harmony with your surroundings and yourself, as well as how to deal with the different phases of your life. As a green, natural religion, Divine Humanity stresses the interconnection of all things and emphasizes respect for nature. As a religious philosophy, it adheres to the Pythagorean cosmological axioms: "as in the greatest, so in the least"; "as above, so below."

Divine Humanity does not play the unjust and inequitable religious game of a patriarchal sexual identity (sun worship) or matriarchal (moon worship) but is a religion and philosophy of the stars. A religion of equality and justice—social and racial justice. Divine Humanity supports and believes in "choice" and reproductive justice.[38]

As a religious philosophy, Divine Humanity allows each one of us to fully participate in life without the divisive aspects of religious creed, dogma, or doctrine. There is no orthodox theology. We each have the freedom to express ourselves in whatever manner we chose in dress, head covering, or our partner in a relationship. And no dietary restrictions: yes, you can enjoy an aged single malt scotch or hot coffee in the morning. Always keep in mind the three maxims inscribed in the Temple of Apollo at the ancient oracle site of Delphi, Greece: *Know Thyself*, *Nothing in Excess*, and *Keep the Measure*. Freedom – a life of freedom.

The Absolute – The One

Please use common sense. There are eight billion plus galaxies. Within each, there are an unknown number, probably billions, of stars. This is known creation. The earth sits in the corner of one of these galaxies—the Milky Way. It is the height of folly and arrogance that any human being or religious institution would have intimate knowledge and be able to identify and label the Creator of our known universe within their concrete of dogma and doctrine.

In fact, the dogmatic and doctrinal issue of "my god versus your god" has caused an unknown amount of suffering and bloodshed over the millennia.

Divine Humanity acknowledges that the One, the Creator, the Unknown-the Uncreated, cannot be identified or imagined in human terms, just in Absolute terms, as One. It is the Greatest Mystery of all

Mysteries. Divine Humanity uses the term God when referring to the Absolute, the One.

However, Divine Humanity is not referring to the concept of the Christian God—the Father, Son and the Holy Ghost, but to the Absolute - the One, Creator, greatest Mystery of Mysteries, the Divine, the All, the Concealed and the Revealed, which is both immanent and transcendent and beyond human comprehension. "According to Plato, the One is the term most suitable for defining the Absolute, since the whole precedes the parts and diversity is dependent on unity, but unity not on diversity. The One, moreover, is before being, for to be is an attribute or condition of the One."[39]

Thus God, the One and Oneness of all, the Mystery of Mysteries, which is within us and that is outside of us, transcends our abilities even as divine human beings to comprehend the essence of what is the greatest mystery of all. God surpasses our dualistic view of reality and is neither male nor female but is the Mystery of all that there is. God is One, love not fear, immanent, and transcendent.

The Revealed

Each of us and all other things are not an image but a reflection, the revealed, of God. A rose by any other name is still a rose just as God by any other name is still the One—the greatest Mystery of mysteries. The Mystery is unexplainable and *concealed*. But the reflection of God is known and is awesome in its simplicity, complexity, and immensity—portrayed by a beautiful collage of creations ranging from cedar trees, bumble bees and humans to stars, galaxies, and black holes. This is the Intrinsic Relative of the Reflective Absolute. This is total inclusiveness. This is the Absolute, as Revealed—the Reflective Absolute, which is within all Relative things of Creation. The universe is both One and Many—Unity in Multiplicity.

Worldview: Radical Non-duality—Our Oneness[40]

Our sacred self and our profane self are non-dual and interpenetrate; as well, all other sentient beings' sacred identity and profane identity are non-dual and interpenetrate—permeate each other. This is true Oneness.

Divine Humanity believes that the relative world of our everyday experience and the absolute world of the Divine are inseparable aspects of a single reality. The relative and absolute are non-dual. Oneness means that the body and mind are non-dual. Because of the fusion of body and mind the attainment of Awakening is not affected in the mind alone but is also equally realized in the body.

Spirit and Matter are not separate from each other but interpenetrate. "Christ taught that the Kingdom of God is within us. What does this mean? The kahunas[41] teach the same thing! Within us are both Spirit and Matter. We must know them both. All the powers of the kahunas, to heal, to control nature, to bless, and to curse, are based on this one secret....

"What does it mean to combine the Spiritual and the Material? What does it mean, 'Know thyself?' Some people are only materialistic. They become weak when they lose health and wealth. Others try to be only spiritual. They become weak when they are impractical. Both types of people have no real foundation. Life is a blending of spirituality with sensible materialism."[42]

An Indigenous Consciousness is a consciousness of interpenetrative radical nonduality—a oneness of being.

Radical Nonduality states that Principle (Heart) and Knowledge (Mind) are nondual. Macrocosmically, Principle is the entire cosmos – Knowledge is the Divine Consciousness that permeates and interpenetrates the entire cosmos. The unseen world and the seen world are not opposed or separated but are two aspects of a single reality.

Our Indigenous Consciousness sees a reality where there is no separation between mind and body, dark and light, or spirit and matter. The most profound and essential nature of things is not distinct from the things recognizable by our senses. In other words, our sacred self and our profane self are nondual and permeate each other; likewise, all other sentient beings' (things') sacred identities and profane identities are nondual and interpenetrate. This is true oneness. And we may awaken to this Indigenous Consciousness while still alive in this imperfect and corruptible body and mind.

With an Indigenous Consciousness our awareness and perception of nature, where us and all things are interconnected not separate, results in a *participatory consciousness*. In other words, we experience a oneness with nature knowing that we are within nature and nature is within us. This is known as *participation mystique*, which is a direct spiritual-religious experience with the totality of body-mind and not just the intellect. It is an immersion in the mysteries of nature and the seeking of knowledge through mystical participation. This may be as simple as sitting alone under a tree and listening to the sounds of nature and our own heart or as complex as dawn bathing in a stream or ocean.

Love – Heart – Divine Consciousness

Our heart contains love. Love in its purest form means Oneness—blending of spirit and matter. Our heart is where our divine spark and radical nondualistic consciousness (divine consciousness) is located. However, our spark (fire of the divine) and our divine consciousness are dormant. Until they are both awakened, our dualistic consciousness in the brain dominates our thoughts, reality, and worldview. When our left - right hemispheres are merged, visualize a rainbow bridge of consciousness, our divine spark, our radical nondualistic consciousness (love), awakens in our heart. This is heart-love, the luminous light of our divine spark. Once awakened we bring this divine light of our heart to all others and to all things of the earth.

Since we are human beings on earth, once awakened we still need to maintain a dualistic consciousness. When we awaken, we do not loss our dualistic consciousness. It remains in our brain/mind while our divine consciousness is awakened in our heart. This means that our thoughts, actions, and words flow from our heart through our mind.

As it is said, "our heart is the best compass we have." From our heart, we speak truth, express forgiveness, compassion, and empathy for others. Our eyes view equality, not inequality, and recognizes the sacredness of nature. Heart-love is the love of nature with the knowledge and understanding that whatever we do to nature, we do to ourselves.

The word love is easy to banter around and as a talking point in promoting books and workshops. Throw in forgiveness and suddenly you have become spiritual enlightened. But love in its purest meaning of oneness is difficult to practice. And it is even more difficult to embody this heart-love of oneness in the inner core of one's self and in one's soul.

One last point: Keep in mind that even though awakened, we are still human, have a dualistic consciousness and at various times will still express dysfunctional human traits such as anger.

Light

Light may be seen as a symbol of the Divine—Eternal Light. This is the Divine light/spark/fire. Fire is the process of liberating the energy hidden in a log or wood or a lump of coal. Divine light permeates all things: space, humans, trees, stones, animals, even the most insignificant. We cannot see the Divine, but we become aware of Divine's presence when we see the beauty of the world, when we look into the eyes of a baby, and when we experience love of others, nature, and all things of the earth.

Quantum Computing—Radical Nonduality

Years ago, before quantum computing, I approached two of my martial arts students about one of my suppositions. One was an engineer and other a computer "geek." I mentioned to them my theory of computing. Instead of a dualistic binary system of 1s and 0s, I proposed a radical nonduality paradigm of blending 1 with 0. In other words, at the same time. Interesting enough, when you blend a 1 and 0, it turns into the symbol for *phi* (Φ)!

Traditional computers utilize individual bits, which store information as binary 0 and 1 states. Quantum computers rely on quantum bits, or qubits. Qubits can represent numerous possible combinations of 1 and 0 at the same time. In other words, a blending of 1 and 0.

"Thanks to this counterintuitive phenomenon, a quantum computer with several qubits in superposition can crunch through a vast number of potential outcomes simultaneously. The final result of a calculation emerges only once the qubits are measured, which immediately causes their quantum state to 'collapse' to either 1 or 0."[43] It seems that measuring, a function of dualistic consciousness, causes the quantum radical nondualistic state to collapse. So, the question for scientists and engineers is how to measure while keeping the quantum radical nondualistic state intact.

Burning Water

The awakening quest in life is to wash by fire and burn by water. This is a metaphor, and a reality, of the joining or blending of the two opposite elements of purification symbolizing a state of radical nonduality. Symbolically, this merging of fire and water represents spirit permeating matter. And, "there is proof that the dynamics of the union of two opposites is at the basis of all creation, spiritual as well as material."[44]

To awaken our spark within our bodies composed of approximately 60% water requires a prolong period of our sacrifice of our self-to-our self (awakening) to release the fire within where it merges with our watery body—an interpenetration of spirit and matter.

There is a power, a force that is the single, dynamic, sacred power or energy that is the unifying totality of all things— a universal life force. It is in constant movement, eternally self-generating and self-regenerating while encompassing and interpenetrating the whole cosmos. It is immanent and at the same time transcendent. This power on a personal level is the inner heat generated by the shaman released during ascetic practice.

A balance between the merging of spirit and matter is the "key to life"—to a life lived in love and power. "The body 'buds and flowers' only when the spirit has been through the fire of sacrifice; in the same way the Earth gives fruit only when it is penetrated by solar heat, transmuted by rain. That is to say, the creative element is not either heat or water alone, but a balance between the two."[45]

One more point: We may consider that fire represents knowledge that burns away the defilement of ignorance while water represents compassion that washes away the passions.[46] Blended together we overcome ignorance while vanishing our defiling passions.

Passing-Over and Reincarnation

What happens after we physically die? Divine Humanity believes that we "pass-over" to the heavenly realms. Our human bodies are mortal, but our soul is immortal. Divine Humanity believes in reincarnation and that there is consciousness in the heavenly realms.

Each one of us has a heavenly lineage—a heavenly DNA (based on previous lives) and an earthly lineage—parental DNA. With this belief, racial prejudice has no relevance or foothold. "In the ancient world, the metaphysical views of the immortality of the soul and reincarnation often went hand in hand. The one was seen, in some ways, to justify the other as may be observed as major subjects in Plato's *Meno, Timaeus*, explicitly described in *Republic X* and elsewhere."[47]

Two Lineages

There are two bloodlines. Every Divine Human has not only an ancestral line of the earth but in addition has an angelic lineage of the heavens. Of course, our earthly bloodline flows from our parent's ancestral lines while our heavenly evolution stems from our previous incarnations. It is easier to track our earthly bloodline, but our angelic ancestry is much more difficult to know, to accept and to understand. With this belief you can truly see that we are, in one way or another, each other's brother and sister.

Each of us has two lineages. This is one of the reasons why there is emotional confusion surrounding the fetus and life. I have had people in their attempt to prove that the fetus is a living person state that their baby in the womb responded to various styles of music Of course, there is an emotional attachment to the feelings of having life growing within you. Yes, it is alive just as the heart of the mother is alive. Yet, it is not a soulful human being at this point in time. It is developing its earthly DNA lineage. It is a potential human being as it has not yet interpenetrated with its soulful heavenly lineage. This occurs at birth with the first breath of life, the cry, and the descent of the heavenly DNA—the Golden Dew.

Unity in Multiplicity

The cosmos, the seen and unseen, is both the "one and many." To the ancient Greeks, Apollo represented this principle of unity and Dionysus represented this principle of multiplicity. Apollo was the unity of the *Sun behind the sun* and Dionysus was manifestation. "Like the Egyptians, for whom the physical sun was a symbol of the one -transcendent God of which the other gods were attributes, the Greeks were aware of the fact that in order for creation to exist, the principle of Unity must necessarily express itself in Diversity. As it is with the universe, so it is with the soul; as archetypal psychology has shown, the soul is a differentiated unity, populated by a variety of principles and archetypes. When these principles become harmonically balanced in the song of life, then the soul attains the power of unified expression. But without a diversity of notes the unity of melody becomes impossible. That is why the Greeks (and their later admirers in the Renaissance) recognized the reality of the various divinities who are subordinate to the One."[48]

As a religious belief, this premise of the "one and many" extends as far back as the ancient Egyptians and Greeks. The Egyptians' numbering sequence began with one, not zero. They felt that "zero represents a nothingness, an absence, and implies that something does not exist and for the Egyptians everything *is*—even Chaos, the negation, *is*."[49] In other words, "the great Unity, the number One is the totality of all existence; all things are One in essence, and love is the cohesive force that makes possible the recognition of all the parts."[50]

MORNING STAR

"The herald of the light is the morning star. This way man and woman approach the dawn of knowledge, because in it is the germ of life, being a blessing of the eternal." –Haji Ibrahim of Kerbala

"Imagine a world of Love."
Imagine was a song by John Lennon that asked us to imagine a world without divisive religion.

After the pandemic, organized religion needs to go the way of the Dodo bird. At the beginning of the pandemic some churches defied the stay-at-home order and social distancing rules of governors and consequently spread the virus. In California, health officials in Sacramento tried to get members of Bethany Slavic Missionary Church, where at least 70 congregants have been infected, to stop gathering in private homes for Bible studies. Bible study: religious truth and guidance is not to be found in the Bible but in nature, in the sun and moon, in the stars of heaven, and within our heart.

In my estimation The Bible, the "book," has brought more chaos, destruction, separateness, pain, and suffering than it has unity, love, and forgiveness. The "book" seemingly overrides common sense and experience. Add to this the realization that the Bible is a translated copy of words and teachings spoken ages ago. According to Newsweek, "No television preacher has ever read the Bible. Neither has any evangelical politician. Neither has the pope… At best, we have all read a bad translation—a translation of translations of translations of hand-copied copies of copies of copies of copies, and on and on, hundreds of times." Not only do we have inaccurate translations, but we have something even more sinister—manipulation for agendas of power and control. The Living Bible, for example, says Jesus "was God"—even though modern translators pretty much just invented the words.[51]

Thief in the Night[52]

God is the One, God is Love, the Unknown, the All, the Great Mystery, the Uncreated, the Sun behind the sun beyond human's consciousness to know— no group or religion can claim God, the One, solely as its own.
—Rev. Dr. JC Husfelt

I make these statements out of my soul's truth as I am the Morning Star and I am a religious revolutionary- a heretic to organized religion. Working outside the box of established religious dogma and doctrine, a religious revolutionary is rarely seen by the masses and is usually likened to the proverbial thief in the night.

In October of 1993, my wife, Sher, and I journeyed to the Big Island of Hawaii leading a group of spiritual seekers. It was here where I experienced the divine call, both as something heard and something seen in the form of a vision and a voice. My vision occurred in the pre-dawn when I saw a star shining brighter than any other and the voice from heaven said: "This star is you; you are this star; the purification is of the people; all are one." The star was Venus as the Morning Star. This is the star of the morning which rises into the mind, clear and conceptual light.[53] As the herald of the dawn, the one who comes with the dawn, a dawn bather[54]—I am the Morning Star.

When I was born during the Chinese Year of the Fire Dog, Venus was in its evening star phase. I am both morning star and evening star—twin symbology. The evening star of my birth reflects my past life revealed by the Visitation, while the morning star is the energetic symbology of my present incarnation.[55]

Tulum: Temple of the Descending God August 1987

In Nahual mythology, *Quetzalcóatl*[56] is identified with Venus as the morning star and *Xolotl* as the evening star. In Tulum, north of Yucatan, over the door of the *Temple of the Descending God* is a descending star image symbolizing *Xolotl* meaning both dog and twin. *Sahagun*, Franciscan missionary, relates that the dog is a sign of fire and states that this fire is of celestial origin. In addition, *Xolotl* is represented falling from the sky, carrying a torch. *Xolotl's* exclusive mission is to carry the spark from which he is carrier to the other end of the world.

Shamanic/Spiritual Medicine Power

As authentic shamans, Sher and I are blessed to be two of those who still practice and "initiate" people into bathing. This "initiation" is not one of membership, but one of death and resurrection/rebirth. One of the spiritual/shamanic lineages/traditions that we hold is the Canadian Northwest First People Coast Salish. We were passed-on this spiritual medicine, the power, and authority of bathing, burnings ("feeding the spirits"), and shamanic healing after a long apprenticeship with Mom and Vince Stogan, revered spiritual healers and Indian

Doctors (shamans) of the Coast Salish – Musqueam Indian Band. Our tales of bathing's, burnings, and healings and other shamanic initiations, experiences and Otherworldly visitations are told in our memoirs: *Tequila and Chocolate*.

OTHERWORLD

The Otherworld is real and is blended with our world; there is no separation, just a oneness of essence. Many people approach the Otherworld (spirit world) from a dualistic perspective. Usually, their consciousness pictures a hierarchy, as "up there somewhere" in relationship to the Earth. From a Christian dualistic hierarchical standpoint, Heaven is up, and Hell is down, and after physical death, you end up for eternity in one or the other. While alive, the only link you have to Heaven is through the Church and their priests and ministers. There is no direct spiritual link for the faithful. The Church is the gatekeeper. Contrary to this Christian drivel based on greed and power, Divine Humanity prescribes to a nonhierarchical reality where the Otherworld and the universe blend together as one. Our hope is to awaken people to awareness of the Otherworld and the perennial mystical knowledge that experiences the unity of the universe that blends with the diversity perceived by our senses.

The Visitation: Revealing Who We Were In A Previous Lifetime

The Divine Light of the angels during the day.

Sher and I know the Otherworld—the truth of the Otherworld. We do not have faith in the Otherworld; We do not believe in the Otherworld; We know the Otherworld. To have faith or to believe a thing does not make it true. "If you are blind and have never seen the sun rise it does not matter how many hypotheses you can array, you still don't know. Belief is simply the adoption of someone else's idea. Once you have seen the sun you do not believe in it, you know it."[57]

We have been in the presence of otherworldly beings, which my wife identified as angels, but they just as well could have been identified as gods or goddesses. No matter what identity is assigned, most importantly, we have not seen angels in our mind, in a cloud formation, or in our dreams or as some type of human figure. We have been in the presence of and witness to an archangel and two assisting angels as three massive pillars of living translucent-ethereal light.[58] The archangel was *Mikaël*, known to most as the Archangel Michael.

Having been in their presence, we know angels in the same way that we know a sunrise, the buzz of a bee, or rain falling on our head. We know otherworldly beings not with our mind but with our senses—no filters. It was a sensory firsthand experience

The term I use for this unprecedented event is the Visitation. It occurred on the night of the new moon, Sunday, August 3, 1997, in the woods of Maine. Early on that Sunday afternoon, we experienced an otherworldly storm. One moment, the sky was crystal clear, tinged only with a few clouds, and in the next moment, the sky darkened into an ominous, swirling bluish-black tempest. There was a moment as if the world paused—there was no sound or movement as if a giant were holding its breath. And then...thunder, lightning, and rain. Torrents of rain fell as thunder boomed overhead and lightning struck all around my wife, me, and our twelve apprentices.

At the time, we did not know what to make of such an unusual natural occurrence. Approximately eight hours later, with the appearance of an archangel and two assisting angels, as three immense pillars of light, the reason for the storm became apparent. The volume and intensity of the thunder and rain and the strength and force of the lightning was a purification of the earth and its elements. A major sanctification had taken place.

It is interesting to note that three months before the Visitation, we far traveled to Cornwall, the sacred land of King Arthur and Michael:

Both are different versions of Sun-Gods, ruling the high places and the destiny of the land. Both are to return, victorious, at the time of the second coming. Michael, leader of the heavenly hosts, according to the apocryphal message in the Book of Enoch, 20.55: "holds the secrets of the mighty Word by which God created heaven and Earth."[59] That Word is Love:

"Love is central to life. It is a binding force between a parent and their [sic] child and one divine human being to another divine human being. Love may be sexual, and possibly, emotional and physical intimacy. However, the foundational meaning and essence of Love is Oneness – unity.

"Ahavah means 'love' in Hebrew. The Jewish mystics remark on the affinity between the word ahavah, 'love,' and 'echad,' one. The numerical value of their letters is the same: 13.

"Oneness, unity, is the aspiration of love, and love emerges from a perception of unity. This insight is also expressed in the Shema: its first line declares God's unity and ends with the word 'echad.' Then follows the mitzvah to love God. Love comes out of a sense of God's unity pervading all things.

"There are three commands to love in the Torah; 'Love your neighbour as yourself ' (Leviticus 19:18); 'Love the stranger as yourself ' (Leviticus 19:34); and 'You shall love the Lord your God for all your heart, soul and strength' (Deuteronomy 6:4)."[60]

The Picture: Lights during the Day

On an October afternoon of the same year, one of our apprentices contacted me. "JC, you'll never guess what I have," he said in an excited tone. "While you were finishing the late-afternoon building of the death spiral, I took a picture of you in the center of it. When I got home, I just threw the camera into my truck. Last week, I finally got around to getting the pictures developed. I knew something was up when the photo shop lady said, 'One of your pictures has caused quite a stir.'"

Photo Jim Kalnins taken during the completion of building the Death Spiral.

"Guess what?" he continued. "I have a daylight photograph of the archangel and the two assisting angels. They were observing us building the (death) spiral, and no one ever suspected!" The picture is sacred and precious. It revealed a very faint image of what looks like the shape of a sword (a sword of light) or an elongated star pointing to the heavens. This dim image is within the center of the reflected light. This is the picture at the beginning of the story and above.

The full story of the Visitation and many other direct experiences of the Otherworld as well as this world are told in our memoirs:

Tequila and Chocolate, The Adventures of the Morning Star and Soulmate:A Memoir.

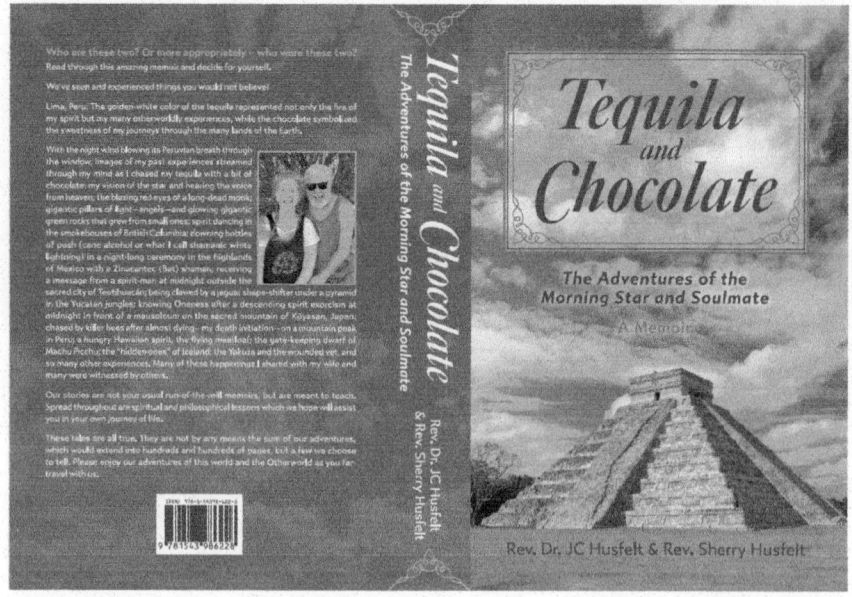

AWAKENING

Fundamental awakening is "a way of collapsing the distance between mind and enlightened mind, and thus, abolishing the dualism that is itself the stuff of delusion."[61]

One of the foundations of spiritual evolution lies in altruistic growth since the energy of evolution is the energy of Love.

Our Seven Steps are a beginning voyage into the deep mystery of yourself and everything else. It is *a mysterium*, a mystery, *tremendum et fascinans*—tremendous, horrific, as it may shatter your fixed notions of things, and at the same time utterly fascinating, because it's authentic life.

With the dawn of each day I take another step on this journey of life that at certain times is mysterious, maybe magical, sometimes mundane, and at times—interesting. Interesting is a term that I use to represent the ebb and flow of life—the times that are trying and a struggle to our spirit and soul such as this pandemic. All three are experiences of life that we need to go through for our awakening.

In our journey of spirit, we must embrace the mysteries of the earth and heaven for transformation. We need to experience the moment to moment magic of life. We need to laugh and discover joy, possibly within the simple things of life, and release the burdens that accumulate from the interesting times of our life's passage.

Awakening is a life journey of love and the heart. Stupidity, fear, greed, arrogance, ignorance, and materialistic worship are a few of our barriers and hindrances to our awakening that we need to release.

We are on a journey of heart. It is a search for truth as well as a quest for the ultimate reality of wholeness or oneness. It is a passage into the unknown. A key component of our quest is courage. It takes courage to step into the unknown and to think outside the box of mundane life. And then, it requires a courageous spirit to trust in a journey of life that few others are willing to take.

Our path is one that few choose because they have an un-enlightened or a "covered" heart. This is a "blind heart;" a heart that is stupid, fearful, spiritually ignorant, dogmatic, dualistic, egotistic, and materialistic. By contrast, the ones who are fearless, open, and striving towards a oneness of spirit have a "heart that sees." It is a heart that is crystal clear—a sparkling mirror reflecting the spirit of heaven and earth. It is our inner still-pond, reflecting the purity of the moon of our souls. Our goal: the blending of heart and mind, the union of all-encompassing love and profoundest knowledge.

Reflection

What motivated early mystics was a desire to come nearer to self-awareness and, thus, to God. Mathematics was a tool of language through which harmony could be expressed, and as these early mystics knew, divinity and harmony are one. To them God was unity, and how else but through proportion could creation reflect the creator?[62]

All things reflect the Divine, the Absolute. This is first knowledge. As part of this first knowledge, the astonishing idea evolved that the divine spark of our own intelligence (mind and consciousness) was a part of a greater Intelligence (divine mind and consciousness), just as our body, in common with trees, stones, plants, animals, the stars, in other words, the "universe" (the Relative) itself, was part of the reflection.

Current research has shown that "in set theory, the reflection principle states that every conceivable property of the Absolute (the class of all sets) is also part of any given set. In other words, every conceivable property of the Absolute is shared by the Relative."[63]

According to Plato, the universe reflects *Logos*. In the myth of the *Timaeus*, "Plato depicts the World Soul as being divided according to the ratios of perfect harmony: the exemplar of the physical cosmos is itself the harmonic blueprint, 'the Logos,' on which all creation is based."[64]

Furthermore, this first knowledge was discovered by the ancient Greeks, "when mathematical philosophers noticed that no matter how many times one (Absolute) is multiplied by itself the result is always one, a significant question was raised: How does one (Absolute) become the many? Their answer was… as a reflection."[65]

In other words, the universe is reflective in nature and is both One and Many. If our mind and heart are as clear as a dust-free mirror, and we recognize the One and Many aspects of ourselves, then our innermost desires and our true destiny will be achieved. However, for many of us, our reflection, our mirror, is dirty and clouded by an unresolved past. When our reflection lacks brilliance, the result is a dullness of spirit where our spark remains un-awakened and that light of God within us is nowhere to be seen. We need clarity of self. To achieve this, we need to wipe our slate and mind-mirror clean by cleansing our past through forgiveness. This generates a compassionate spirit that lets us see others in a totally different light—not one of fear but one of love. This is the beginning stage of our awakening and transformation of self; the remaking of ourselves as divine humans.

Awakening our starlight/divine fire/divine spark is the grand journey of being human—becoming the divine light and shining it on others.

Six Great Elements

Six is the hexagram or 6-pointed star symbolizing the marriage, the union, of the spiritual and the physical, the vertical fusion of spirit and matter, of human and divine. Divine Humanity prescribes to six great elements that interpenetrate and are in eternal union. Six is the first number of perfection. The world was created in six days. "Order involves numbers, and among numbers by the laws of nature, the most suitable to productivity is 6, for if we start with 1, it is the first perfect number, being equal to the product of its factors (i.e. 1 x 2 x 3) as well as made up of the sums of them (i.e. 1 + 2 + 3)."[66]

The first five elements are earth, water, fire, air or wind, and space. These five elements are physical as well as metaphysical (e.g., water equals ocean, and emotion equals water). The sixth great element, which interpenetrates the other five, is consciousness. This belief opens worlds of opportunity, knowledge, and the wisdom that form is inseparable from mind and the mind is inseparable from form—a nonduality or oneness. And we realize that we are never alone or out of touch. Everything has a consciousness that is connected in a web of life extending out and back to the farthest star in the most distant galaxy.

The term "sixth sense" would be a node to our sixth element of consciousness, Divine Mind, which interpenetrates all things of the seen and unseen cosmos. Knowing things that others do not know, would seem like—magic.

One further point concerning first knowledge. The concept of six elements extends as far back as the Ancient Egyptians. They identified the six elements as air, earth, water, fire, darkness, and light. Darkness relates to our element of space and light correlates with our sixth element of Divine Mind.

Out of the Void—Space[67]

In a few religious and secular philosophies, our fifth element space would be called the void, meaning nothingness. Contrary to this, my cosmological and ontological theory on being and creation does not view void as a nothingness. It states: "From the Absolute and its reflection, Reflective Absolute, was 'birthed the duality that was nondual'—a void that was not void."[68] I continue theorizing: "Divine Humanity refers to the absolute and the reflective absolute as the great silence (the sound of the Hebrew letter aleph is silence), not the big bang, and the duality that was nondual as the dark ocean—containing the eternal male and eternal female. Continuing on, the reflective absolute (divine mind and consciousness) now interpenetrates this voidless void (dark ocean), and creation occurs."[69]

But what does it mean when I write, "A void that was not void and voidless void?" I was alluding to the energetic/vibrational response of the Absolute reflecting itself—the Reflective Absolute. This resulted in a duality that was nondual, a void not a void, an emptiness not empty that was filled with power containing the energy/vibrational potential of the Absolute. I go on to state: "From this the reflective absolute and the dark ocean (in triple aspect)[70] birth the great sea—the relative universe (seen and unseen). The great sea has wave action or vibration."[71] It is at this point that the voidless void becomes the fifth element space.

The latest research according to Harold Puthoff, PhD, the vacuum of space is a "plenum." Space is a fullness of energetic potentialities in balance. This equilibrium prevents the enormous energy potentials from becoming actual, which therefore appears as a void or a vacuum. But every point in empty space, is a locus of convergence of humongous energies, coming from all directions simultaneously, balancing them out. At any point where there is an imbalance or asymmetry in this omnidirectional canceling of energies, there appears a disturbance known as matter. Following on this, according to physicist Nassim Haramein, "what we think of as solid matter is more than 99 percent 'space' — energy. This 'space' is not nothingness, but infinite potential. On an atomic level, god is within us."

In other words, what this verifies is the divine potential, the infinite potential that each of us have closer at hand than we have ever realized—a divine awakening within us, blended with the developmental potential of human perfection.

Magic

The true magic in the universe is "love and its opposite is hatred"—Empedocles

Divine Humanity acknowledges that the Creator, the Unknown and the Uncreated, cannot be identified or imagined by the human mind and cannot be put into human terms, just in absolute terms, as it is the greatest mystery of all mysteries. The Absolute—the One— which Divine Humanity refers to as God, is beyond form and conception, the unmanifest. It is outside of time and space; in a sense it is timelessness. For reasons beyond what any human mind may comprehend, the Absolute reflected itself—the Reflective Absolute. The monad reflected itself such as revealed by the Fibonacci series where each progressed number is the sum of the two previous ones i.e. 1, 1, 2, 3, 5, 8, 13, 21 and so forth. The Pythagoreans believed that One (first 1 or Absolute) was not a number at all but gave birth to all numbers.

* * *

How does all this point us to magic? The cosmos, seen and unseen, is reflective. It then makes sense that magic is a natural phenomenon due to the reflective nature of the universe as it responds to human thoughts, words, desires, and aspirations.

Because of the magical, reflective nature of reality, awareness is required to attract what is desired. People who do not know what they want, usually attract what they need. This may be a seemingly random series of situations and perhaps unhappy events, destined to jolt them to a higher level of awareness in the long run. Since the universe does respond to our innermost desires, true philosophers have always held that one should be idealistic in spirit and perpetually aim to invoke the highest. As you journey through the seven steps be positive and enthusiastic in word, deed, heart, mind, and spirit.

Nevertheless, there is one most important point in awakening. We know due to the reflective cosmos that magic does work. However, there may be barriers to our magical success. These obstacles are our flaws and woundings' within ourselves—a prime reason to "know yourself." We must face and then heal/transform them. There is one other "wild card" to understand. We have free will, but it intertwines with and is threaded through our tapestry of life with our fate and destiny. And all are interwoven with divine will. The Pythagoreans would view this concept as the process of universal order.

* * *

Furthermore, there is the most important concept of cosmic sympathy, "something like 'action and reaction in the universe.' All creatures, all created things, are united by a common bond."[72] This was first "formulated by the Stoic philosopher Posidonius of Apamea (ca. 135—ca. 50 B.C.), called 'the Rhodian' after the island where he taught. His concept implies that anything that happens in any part of the universe can affect something else in the universe, no matter how distant or unrelated it may seem. The idea itself must be incredibly old and predates the concept of causality. It is fundamental for magic, astrology, and alchemy.

"What is called 'sympathetic' magic is based on three principles: similarity (like acts on like); contact (things that touch each other influence each other and may exchange their properties); and contrariety (antipathy works like sympathy). Together, these principles, though they seem partly contradictory, offer explanations to the *magus*, the astrologer, and the alchemist.

"Other ways to describe the workings of cosmic sympathy are 'Inside is like outside' or 'What is above is like what is below.' The whole idea involves a constant exchange of energies between the outside world (the macrocosm, the universe) and the inside world (the microcosm, the psyche). Everything around us can be used to our advantage, if we just know how to 'plug' into the potential that is there."[73]

Two millennium later, the late physicist David Bohm (1917 – 1992), a colleague of Albert Einstein, theorized Posidonius' cosmic sympathy as a new reality of the universe. This reality he named the Implicate Order—the hidden aspect of the universe. "The theory of the Implicate Order contains an ultra-holistic cosmic view; it connects everything with everything else. In principle, any individual element could reveal 'detailed information about every other element in the universe.' The central underlying theme of Bohm's theory is the 'unbroken wholeness of the totality of existence as an undivided flowing movement without borders.'"[74] In other words, "within the Implicate Order everything is connected; and, in theory, any individual element could reveal information about every other element in the universe."[75]

Strong Mind, the Brain, and Consciousness

The totality of the interactions of the mind, brain, and consciousness are mysterious and seldom considered. Each in themselves is an area of mystery. Adding to these are the mysteries of our DNA and genetic makeup, which makes life a playground of seeking knowledge into our being of "who we are."

Knowing ourselves, self-knowledge, means exploring and understanding our consciousness, our mind, and our brain and their effect on our DNA and genetic makeup. With the debilitating effects of our culture and environment on our minds and brains, the scourge of brain-linked ailments is rampant in our society. A scourge which may be reduced and repealed. But how? With this being said, let us explore our trinity in seeking knowledge of ourselves and solutions to the mental/brain blight.

Brain

The brain is composed of three parts—a "triune brain." At the base of a skull is our reptilian brain and next to it is our paleomammalian brain. Both of these protect the self and the survival of it through any means possible. The reptilian and paleomammalian are two parts with the third part being our present human neomammalian brain.

There is interconnection and interplay between the instinctual responses of the reptilian, the autonomic emotional states of the paleomammalian and the cognitive processes of the neomammalian brain. And that interaction between the three levels is not based primarily on verbal language but on other forms of information gathering and processing such as sounds, symbols, non-language chants, sensory, and spatial input.

Consciousness[76]

Of the three, consciousness is the most mysterious with little thought given to it. Ironically, one of the reasons is our dualistic minds, beliefs, and practices based on science, a dualistic paradigm, which separates itself from spirit. As science cannot quantify consciousness, as it cannot be measured, poked or prodded, which means it takes a backseat to the mind and the brain.

When we consider sacred science or the blending of science and spirit, Consciousness becomes the most important and the foundation of our trinity. Our thoughts and their patterns (mind) flow from our consciousness. This affects our minds, which then affects our brains.

A "loop" is created where mind affects brain, brain affects mind, mind affects brain, and so forth. And one step further, our mind affects our body, our body (heart) affects our mind and so forth. But it all begins with our consciousness.

There are eight stages of consciousness, a ninth consciousness and our awakened state of heart-mind consciousness. But in simplified terms, foundationally there are two: a consciousness of dualism and radical nondualism. A consciousness of dualism is one of separation (either-or) while a radical nondualistic consciousness is one of unity or oneness (a blending together of the binaries).

Of the eight stages of consciousness, the first five are our senses: visual consciousness discerns form, hearing consciousness discerns sounds, taste conscious discerns taste, smell consciousness discerns smells, and touch consciousness discerns tactile sensations. Our five sense consciousness's are essential to the overall health of our bodies, minds, and spirits and the awakening of our divine starlight. You may see the Pandora effect of the unbridled technological advances based solely on capitalist gain without concern for the totality of the wellbeing of people's bodies, minds, and spirits. The bottom line: humanity's sensory consciousness is deadening, affecting people's sense of reality, common sense, and connection to the earth and nature.

The next stage after sense consciousness is the one where we will focus our attention: mind and thought consciousness—conscious mind. After mind and thought consciousness is storehouse consciousness (subconscious - 1st Attention then 2nd Attention), then we have supraconsciousness - soul consciousness.

Mind – Thought: Conscious Mind

Our conscious mind is based on either dualism or a blending of dualistic and radical nondualistic consciousness. For the majority of people, their worldview is dualism—separation of the binaries such as male and female, spirit and matter, the brain's right hemisphere and the brain's left hemisphere. Take a moment and ponder how this consciousness feeds the fires and flames of tribalism, sexism, and racism to name just a few resulting from a mindset of dualism. Dualism is the realm of the unhealthy ego (solely focused on the I), which constantly seeks external power, safety, and security. Our minds and thought consciousness are our decision makers, and the ongoing, prevalent decision that we make is where we focus our attention. Many times, the focus of our attention will be based on our concept of power. The majority of ones with a dualistic consciousness view their power externally—not internally of heart and mind with such attributes as unity, courage, kindness, and compassion. One example of seeking external power is through a connection/support of a sports team by wearing their merchandise and /or through identifying with "externally" powerful people such as the worship of Trump by wearing his MAGA hats, Trump clothing, and so forth with the personal meaning—I support Trump, I have power too.

* * *

When we awaken within us our divine starlight, our unhealthy egos are transformed into healthy egos, with the "I" in the "we" and the "we" in the "I"—a consciousness of radical nonduality. Even though our unhealthy egos have been transformed into healthy egos, we will still sometimes exhibit traits and behaviors of unhealthy egos—we are humans, not gods or goddesses.

Unity of the binaries only comes from a consciousness of radical nonduality at the point where we are able to blend the two binaries together. To reach a consciousness of oneness or radical nonduality requires a strong mind and the transitional state of heart-mind consciousness.

Strong Mind

Strong Mind: *mind of no mind, the immovable mind.*
Weak Mind: *Too many mind. Mind sword, mind people watch,*
mind enemy. Too many mind.[77]

During and after this pandemic, it is important to keep a strong mind symbolized as a clean, clear, and unclouded mirror. The mind influences our immune system. Our mind affects our body and our body affects our mind. A strong mind is a powerful mind that can maintain total focus on something without doubt, wavering, or mind chatter. A lack of attention is the antithesis of a strong, powerful mind. And a strong mind is a resilient mind. A powerful mind remains unruffled, imperturbable, unattached, and unfettered. Do not let your mind revert to or become a *palace of mirrors*—an uncontrolled mind. According to one of the Grail stories, "the knights find themselves in the palace of mirrors or the 'Chastel Mortel.' When the mirror is cleansed, and the 'Chastel Mortel' seen for what it is, then the way to union and wholeness lies open."[78]

Emotions and Immunity

Over the past decade, research has shown that the emotional and immunological systems share more than a similarity of functions. The immune and emotional systems mirror each other; both the immunological and emotional responses are dynamic and continuously changing. The majority of living beings use both systems to adjust dynamically to the ever-changing conditions of the external environment. Both systems can either be protective for the body if kept under control or detrimental to it when they are in disarray. It has been found that the duration of what we could call an immunological or emotional challenge is a key factor in determining its impact on the emotional or immunological response. **Duration:** Think COVID-19.

They have found that both the emotional and immune systems are highly "plastic," which means the ability to change and adjust continuously depending on the external factors or living conditions. Adopting a healthier diet, developing a strong mind, and ceasing unhealthy habits such as smoking have all been reported to be beneficial for both the emotional and immunological responses.

There are two types of immune cells: innate (extroverted) and adaptive (introverted personality). Adaptive, as it sounds, creates an inner experience of life events, especially if they have been deleterious for the person. This is called immunological memory. Both innate and adaptive immune cells work toward trying to adjust the body to accommodate the requests of the external and the internal environments.

There are five basic personality traits (openness to experience, conscientiousness, extraversion, agreeableness, and neuroticism). Each has specific immunological features or defined susceptibility to immune disorders. Conscientiousness implies a desire to do a task well, to take obligations to others seriously, and an awareness of the impact that their own behavior has on others around them. It has been shown that there is a consistent association between conscientiousness and a reduced inflammatory response.[79] Inflammation is a natural way our bodies fight harmful intruders like viruses. But long-lasting inflammation isn't healthy and could undermine your body's defenses when a real threat arises. Bottom line: be conscientious, wear a mask, social distance, and forgive - heal your past.

The research is not definite yet, but it would seem that a strong mind, the ability to "let-go" and forgive, laughter, the ability to express love and "love thy neighbor," and wellness of body and mind will go a long way in strengthening our immune system and our joy of living.

The mind of no mind, the immovable mind

Following our Seven Steps will help increase the strength of your mind. In ancient japan, there was a concept to strengthen your mind called *fudochi* or "immovable wisdom" meaning immovable spirit or wisdom that cannot be influenced or confused and provides us with a deep sense of clarity and purpose in all our undertakings.

Another concept is *Mushin no shin*— "a mind without mind, a mind of no mind." It seems like a rather paradoxical concept. What it means is a state of mind where our mind is not fixed on or occupied by any thought or emotion. In other words, a person's mind is free from thoughts such as anger or fear.

A concept closely related to *Mushin no shin* is *Fudoshin*. *Fudo* means immovable. *Shin* means spirit, heart, or will. Both together means an immovable heart/spirit/will. It is attained when the mind is totally focused on the totality of sensory input and free of thoughts and emotions - detached but aware and present.

These terms connote a strong mind that is at once firmly in place and yet ever moving. A mind unmoved by carnal temptations. Immobility from the enlightened state is accomplished by maintaining a mind that remains detached, that is, a mind that does not stop or become fixated on any one thing. Combining these concepts, we have the *mind of no mind, the immovable mind.*

In other words, our minds are in the present but at the same time are viewing all aspects of life without the prejudice and woundings of the past coloring our mind when we view people or places of our past. It may be viewed as our heart-mind consciousness.

Kokoro: the heart and its functions; mind and its functions; and center, or essence.
Calligraphy by Dr. Husfelt

Heart-Mind Consciousness

A Mind that Listens and a Heart that Sees – JC Husfelt

Our goal is to blend our heart-mind—the harmony and unity of all-embracing love and deepest knowledge. The mastery of our heart-mind is achievable through rigorous soul-searching and spirit-forging through the confrontation and overcoming of our own fears and weaknesses.

Our heart-mind consciousness is our awakening and awakened minds. It is still corruptible and deluded but awakening to the reality of interpenetrating radical nonduality. It is a shift from viewing life totally from the me (I) position to one where the me (I) and the we interpenetrate—the me in the we, and the we in the me mutually permeate. Keep in mind that even though awakening and awakened, we are still human, have a dualistic consciousness and at various times will still express life from the me position without the consideration of others. We are divine but we are still human.

Our consciousness flows from our hearts through our minds—the sun of our hearts gives light to the moon of our minds. We no longer recognize people by race and gender but as human beings with a divine spark within them. Judgments and discernments are not made on a label of race or sex but based on the person's actions to us and to others.

Storehouse Consciousness: Subconscious

Storehouse Consciousness (body/mind) is the realm of first attention. Just as it implies, this consciousness stores the seeds, and possibly stones, of every moment and experience of our lives, all physical and mental things form our beliefs, assumptions, attitudes, habits, and behaviors. It is our memory bank and follows orders from our mind. Only if the mind is aware and wants to change a response, a pattern, to an outside stimuli. As our body/mind link, it is the depository of all our emotions, habits, and memories. We deposit our mental/emotional wounds (stones) and memories in our bodies. Those wounded pieces that we have not been able to let go of will remain within us physically/energetically until we do so.

Think of it this way, emotions such as anger and happiness occur in our conscious mind, but the resulting feelings remain somewhere in the body. Like a computer, our sub-conscious self-stores all of our memories and experiences and is a co-creator of our reality with our conscious mind and spirit. It is through our conscious minds that we are able to change patterns, to forgive and release our woundings in our subconscious.

* * *

Furthermore, our storehouse consciousness is the location of our instincts and habits. Our habits are based on our beliefs. Habit is all our behaviors held within our subconscious directly or indirectly directed from our conscious mind—learned behavior not instinctive.

Instincts refer to involuntary functions of the body. There are two basic instincts: self-preservation, and survival of the species.

Most importantly, our conscious minds will help transform our storehouse consciousness and its first attention into a second attention. This enables a shift in consciousness of our beliefs, assumptions, and attitudes, which will then change habits and behaviors. To achieve this shift in consciousness, we need to begin shifting our first attention into a second attention, which will then begin a transformation of our conscious minds (thought and mind consciousness—dualistic consciousness) into a heart-mind consciousness (radical nonduality consciousness).

Supraconsciousness: Soul Consciousness

This may be looked at as our guardian angels or our higher selves. It is the divine-spark consciousness that is eternal. Mesoamerican indigenous shamanic cultures refer to this type of consciousness as the tonal of a person. Tonal is the birth guardian or the metaphoric animal twin of the person. Connected with tonal is nagual commonly known as spirit guardian.

In conclusion, do not look at these various states of consciousness as proceeding from sense consciousness to supraconsciousness, but understand that they all interpenetrate, all blend together.

Ninth Consciousness

If there were not a ninth conscious, each of us would be separate from, and not a part of, the web of life—islands isolated unto ourselves. Just as the sixth great element, divine consciousness, interpenetrates the other five elements of space, air, fire, water, and earth (physically and metaphysically), it also interpenetrates our individual eight states of consciousness. Our ninth means that the observer and the observed, self, and other, are not separate but are connected in a oneness of being. We are not our brothers' or sisters' keepers, but we are our brothers or sisters.[80] We are truly one with the divine.

One Step at a Time

After choosing to focus on awakening, patience is required as we need to take one step at a time. Mom and Vince Stogan were the revered spiritual healers of the Coast Salish – Musqueam Indian Band and passed on the tradition to Sher and me. Vince was the fifth generation in his family to carry on the medicine of the smokehouse tradition of initiation and spirit dancing. An insight into Mom and Vince's Salish tradition and culture is the term *skalalitude*. This is being in harmony with nature – a harmonious state of heart and mind where all things are in balance.[81] One of Vince's primary teachings was "one step at a time." The journey of awakening is like climbing a mountain or ladder—one step at a time and take your time at each step. Vince told us that people want to "climb too fast." If you do, there is the possibility that you will fall back down the ladder. If that happens, it will take much longer to get back to where you fell off.

Know the right time.
— Pittacus of Mytilene, 650-570 BC, one of the 7 sages of
Ancient Greece

As we begin this journey of awakening, it would be best to keep a journal account of our journey through this pandemic and our progress in awakening. Please understand that "everything comes in its own time." It will happen in time; we must be patient and trust the process. Patience is a virtue that we need to practice. Spirit and matter are one; the secret is to know the balance of this unity to its time and season. There is a time[82] for everything, and a season for every activity under heaven:

A time to be born and a time to die,
A time to plant and a time to uproot,
A time to kill and a time to heal,
A time to tear down and a time to build,
A time to weep and a time to laugh,
A time to mourn and a time to dance,
A time to scatter stones and a time to gather them,
A time to embrace and a time to refrain,
A time to search and a time to give up,
A time to keep and a time to throw away,
A time to tear and a time to mend,
A time to be silent and a time to speak,
A time to love and a time to hate,
A time for war and a time for peace. (Eccl. 3:1-8)

Awakening is not a quick fix. First you must climb the ladder or Mountain of Initiation, one step at a time and once you reach the seventh step you back down the mountain to step one where you awake to a new self in order to help others and humanity—a responsibility of selflessness.

You will discover as your progress through the steps that our first step *Know Thyself* is the "alpha and omega"—the first is the last and the last is the first. Alpha is contained within omega. In simple terms, alpha and omega means in ancient Hebrew, "the power of new beginnings."

So, after step seven take a brief rest and then repeat the steps in reverse order 7 - 6 - 5 - 4 - 3 - 2 - 1. In other words, *Know Thyself* is the first step and then becomes the last. As you repeat your steps descending back, *Keep the Measure* as the last, now becomes the first. You can see the importance of *Know Thyself* and *Keep the Measure*. In other words, the First Mystery becomes the Last Mystery and the

Last Mystery becomes the First Mystery. Just as the Delphic Apollo was associated with the first and last mysteries, so are we.

The Unknown and Change

Facing the unknown and change is difficult for most people. It is challenging to face up to individual reality; a frankness combined with the desire to change. It can be a painful process for the personality; few people care to look at their failings honestly, and many fear change of any kind as it appears to be a threat to their safety and security. Even so, we ask you to face yourself: to change, to face the unknown, and transform. This pandemic is the perfect time for you to begin awakening. If not now… when?

"Rejoice, O Queen!" they said. "There has been born to you a mighty son." From the sky two pure streams of water fell, refreshing the child and its mother, after which the infant, standing upright, facing east, strode forward **seven steps**, pointed upward with his right hand, downward with his left, and shouted with a noble voice the victory shout of all the Buddhas:

Worlds above, worlds below! The chief in all the worlds am I![83]

SEVEN STEPS
TO AWAKENING

1. KNOW THYSELF

"For he who has not known himself has known nothing,
but he who has known himself has at the same time
already achieved knowledge about the Depth of the All."

– JESUS IN THE BOOK OF THOMAS THE CONTENDER[84]

Sher at the Tholos of Delphi at the Temple of Athena Pronaia, 2006.

To thrive through the pandemic and after, we need to know ourselves. We must ask the question "who am I." The maxim *Know Thyself* (*gnóthi seautón*) or *Get to Know Thyself* is attributed to the Greek Philosopher Chilon of Sparta and was the primary maxim inscribed in the Temple of Apollo (*a* = not, *pollon* = of many) at the ancient oracle site of Delphi, Greece. *Know Thyself* along with the maxim *Nothing in Excess* and the Pythagorean maxim *Keep the Measure* form the foundational heart of the famous and mysterious E of Delphi. E is Zeus' epsilon and "was over the tall gateway entrance to Apollo's temple at Delphi, signifying divine breath or prophecy."[85] Delphi's E is Epsilon (fifth letter of Greek Alphabet)—the ancient secret of Apollo's Temple. The "golden five"—the light that shines out of the darkness.

Furthermore, the E, being the second of seven vowels, represents the second of the seven planets—the sun, which followed the moon in ancient cosmology—and therefore Apollo. Accordingly, the Delphic Epsilon relates to solar rituals, initiations, and primarily our perpetual relationship with "Light - Divine Fire." Awakening our divine fire within begins the process of spreading this light throughout our body. This means our body becomes a luminous vessel of light. We are still very human but have awakened our divine consciousness.

Our heart (sun) and mind (moon) unite within ourselves the power and love of the depth of the night and the light of the day. This is the darkness of all-embracing space and the light of the sun and stars. This is the creative primordial power of life and the luminous all-penetrating power of knowledge. From the blending of these two arises the sacred flame of the enlightened mind/consciousness (*bodhicitta*), which radiates light in which knowledge grows into living wisdom.

In divine providence, salvation is unnecessary, but self-discovery is essential. We do not save that which was lost; we merely discover that which is always there - our divinity.[86]

We do not need the lie of salvation preached by Christianity; the earth does not need its salvation. What each of us needs, notably during this coronavirus, and what the earth needs, is love. Love of self, love of all others, love of the earth and all its creatures, love of the sun and the moon, love of the stars and the heavens—this is the love of God.[87]

* * *

Traditionally, there were two interpretations of this maxim of Know Thyself. The first realizing one's humanity, our functional and dysfunctional self, and the second was recognizing one's essentially divine self. The two combined reveal the original meaning of realizing, recognizing, and honoring one's self, which is first and foremost as a Divine Human. Furthermore, Know Thyself meant "know your divine Nous." Philosophically, Nous, (Greek:"mind" or "intellect") is the aspect of intellectual apprehension and of intuitive thought. It is distinguished from discursive thought and applies to first principles or first knowledge.[88] Additionally, the mind needs to know its own self and feel its union with the divine mind or consciousness.

The Greek philosopher Socrates focused "on how to live in this world. In keeping with the famous admonition at Delphi, 'Know Thyself,' he held that the study of human affairs should be the central topic of philosophic research. Socrates held the people were endowed by the gods with intelligent psuchai, souls, that desired the good. Human beings need to acquire the wisdom through which they can discern the good they desire. Instead, many people fail to attain this wisdom and strive hard after external possessions such as money, social position, etc., which are taken to be good. 'Know thyself' means that one must consciously devote oneself to the understanding of one's own moral nature and to the improvement or purification of one's own soul. This activity is of prime importance in one's life."[89]

Knowing one's self means knowing one's soul—one's divine soul. We are a "child of earth and of starry heaven." Knowing our self, our "self-discovery is a process of self-transformation: progressively taming and refining the disorderly elements of the soul, and "solarizing" one's inner nature by identifying with the author of one's being and its radiant ideals of Justice, Beauty, and the Good. It is upon this fact of the spiritual unity of all beings and things that reposes the basis and foundation of human ethics when these last are properly understood."[90] Yes, we are a child of earth. But most importantly we are the sun (divine) of the Sun behind the sun.[91]

* * *

Awakening to the knowledge of our divine soul is part of the philosophy of Pythagoras. This philosophy "represents a 'purification,' the aim of which is the assimilation to God. The universe is divine because of its order (*kosmos*), and the harmonies and symmetries which it contains and reflects. These principles make the universe divine for they are the characteristics of divinity, and they also innately subsist within the human soul. The Pythagoreans taught that the soul is a harmony. If we are to become like God, then according to Pythagorean philosophy the soul must become aware of its harmonic origin, structure and content."[92]

We contain all principles consisting the greater cosmos (seen and unseen) of which we are a reflection. This includes the powers of divinity. "The problem is not so much of becoming divine as becoming aware of the divine, universal principles within."[93]

It comes down to the knowledge and a knowing of self/soul, the earth, and the heavens—the *kosmos* (universe as beautifully ordered). Knowledge is obtained by observation and is the unifier of subject and object, the known and unknown—a oneness of experience. And from this oneness comes wisdom. As we know ourselves, our true wisdom matures.

Divine Knowledge as Self-Knowledge

Man, know thyself in true proportion.
Oracle of Delphi

Know yourself in order to foresee the future correctly. This self-knowledge was fundamental to the Pythagoreans. They were called "*mathe-matekoi*, which means 'those who study all.' The word *mathema* is the root of the Old English *mathein*, 'to be aware,' and the Old German *munthen*, 'to awaken.' The truths the Pythagoreans sought were the universal truths of self-knowledge and their inquiries relied upon finding an application of these truths in the world around them. The Pythagorean philosophy was based on an attempt to describe the underlying harmony of existence and the nature of the perfect universe in numbers."[94] In other words, be one who studies all cultural spiritual traditions, be aware of all things including your heart and mind, and have the perseverance to awaken.

Knowing ourselves, self-knowledge, means recognizing, first and foremost, that we are Divine Human Beings. Our divine spark interpenetrates our humanness—body, mind and spirit. The Absolute interpenetrates the Relative.

Knowing that we are divine human beings means that we are responsible for our own behaviors and actions. There is no distant and far away deity to blame or to seek some form of dogmatic salvation. Each of us has direct access to the mysteries of heaven (Absolute) and earth (Relative). Furthermore, knowing ourselves means realizing that we were born in divinity not in sin.

The constant counter argument to this philosophical statement that we were born in divinity not in sin is always: "if we have divineness within us, why do humans commit the atrocities (slaughter of adults, children and even babies, rape, torture, needless destruction of the earth and its creatures, etc.) that have happened for millennium?"

The answer is quite simple: "Yes, we are born with a divine spark; but our divineness, the light of God, is un-awakened." Knowing this and the realization that we are still humans with a body, mind, emotion and spirit and we will always have the choice of right-action, wrong action, a combination of both or inaction. In other words, even after we awaken our divineness, we will still make human mistakes and possibly do actions that are not true and right. Knowing ourselves means that we will love, and we will fear; we will struggle and suffer, and we will have joy and happiness; we will live, and we will die. This is knowing ourselves and then striving to become more divine with as little human wrong doing as possible.

Sometimes we must lose our self to know our self—JC

Knowing ourselves is the first step in embracing a spiritual life of love and power. Self-knowledge is the key that opens the gate to the wonders and the healing that is within us and outside of us. After acknowledging that we each have a divine spark within that interpenetrates with our humanness, our next step is to awaken our divineness. This involves knowing our human self in the totality of our past and present such as our wounding's and our behaviors. It involves knowing our beliefs and our rules of life as well as our philosophy of Life and Death. Many times, it may mean changing "who we are," losing the old self to become and know the true self. Maybe the self we have denied for many years, possibly as long ago as our childhood.

This process is an on-going discovery of our self and then accepting the truth that the power is within us to change, to transform and to awaken our divine spark. This "divine golden dew of light" that interpenetrates our DNA needs to be awakened, brightened, brought to the surface and nourished until its radiance suffuses the world. This is our luminous body that grows within and shines without. In so doing, our relationship to ourselves and to all other things of the world is transformed from being based on fear to being based on love.

With this first step, we embrace a life philosophy of to know, to dare, to do and to be silent (non-chattering mind and mouth).

There is another important point. Knowing ourselves means to know the truth of ourselves. This is one reason why True Talk, one of our Pillars of Light, is such an important quality of self. If we are unable to speak our truth to others, how would be able to acknowledge the truth of our own self?

Self-knowledge allows us to untangle ourselves from the illusions of our past. Without fear and/or guilt we are able to separate the essential from the unessential, morally real from the unreal. In other words, we must be authentic and know who we truly are; do not deny your past, your origin of birth, your past woundings, the ones healed and the ones that still cause hurt. Accept that you may have had a broken heart but transform the fear of further woundings to the heart with the strength of love.

Please understand that unconditional love is what we want, but often we are afraid of love without consciously knowing it, and so we may act both blind and deaf to love's presence. The Divine is love. Love is within us and outside us. As we awaken by letting go of fear, uncertainty, and discover our authentic selves, we begin to experience a personal transformation. We start to see beyond our old reality, as defined by the physical senses, and enter a state of clarity in which we discover that inner peace and unconditional love are, in fact, real.

"Those who know others are wise. Those who know themselves are enlightened."[95]

"Most people think they know who they are and would proclaim so without a second thought. In truth, they only know who they are in the context of the given situations and experiences they have been presented with in their lives. They may even carelessly venture in the fallacy of determining themselves according to what they do in life - what profession they exercise. Getting to know one's self is not an easy task, nor is it one accomplished overnight. Most learned men and women would suggest that it takes a lifetime to achieve—perhaps, even longer than that. Knowing one's self doesn't merely consist of acknowledging what our senses feel or what or thoughts register or what our emotions are. Certainly, these are aspects of self-knowledge, but actual knowledge of one's self stems from the understanding of the true causes behind the very Force that gave birth to our being (body and soul) and the forces that keep it motion. Knowing thyself is knowing the harmony of nature and how you co-exist in it; how dependent and interlinked these two are. Knowing the harmony of nature, on the other hand, can never be fully achieved without knowing the harmony of the solar system, nay, the entire cosmos. 'Knowing' is not a process of strictly rational thought. It is also a deep-felt emotion - a vivid, constant experience."[96] Discover this harmony of nature in our third step: *Accept a Green Philosophy: Experience and Embrace the Magic of Mother Nature.*

Astrology[97]

One tool in knowing ourselves involves knowing our birth astrology and most importantly, our ascendant and planets in the first and twelfth house. "In esoteric astrology, the ascendant or rising sign portends the soul's purpose for the incarnation. It tells us what the purpose is and how the soul will seek to accomplish it. Both are revealed in the sign of the ascendant. Therefore, planets on either side of the ascendant (in the twelfth or first house) are particular tools as far as the soul is concerned."[98]

The validity of astrology may be verified by the philosophy of macrocosm and microcosm. This is the premise that all occurrences in the microcosm (humanity/earth) are influenced by the macrocosm (the heavens) and is Greek in origin possibly dating back to the fifth century BCE. Later on, an axiom developed known as "as below, so above; as above, so below."This philosophy[99] taken from *The Emerald Tablet of Hermes Trismegistus* "underpinned the work of the great minds of the past, such as Plato, Aristotle, Pythagoras, and Ptolemy."[100] This proposes that we reflect the heavens. Thus, the manner in which the planets and stars are arranged in heaven when we are born is an imprint and reflection of who we are—a guide to our soul.

Furthermore, "astrology (like the Oracle of Delphi) is one of many tools that can assist us in the task of becoming aligned with our destiny. Astrology's 'map of the soul' (owner's manual) provides each one of us with a map of our inborn potentials and then shows how these inborn potentials will (sooner or later) seek to systemically unfold over the course of our lifetime. As such, in our modern world - too often devoid of meaning - astrology can assist us in purposes of meaning, purpose, self-discovery, soul growth, and being 'brought to completion.'"[101]

Another component of looking to the heavens to reveal essence of self/soul is to be found within fixed stars. "On the day you were born, you not only gained the magic of your horoscope, you also gained the myths and meanings of a sky full of stars. Not all the stars, just those that formed links to your natal planets via what is called parans. By considering the star parans in your life you will be encountering a whole new (though incredibly old) layer of myth and meaning to your chart."[102] And to your soul.

Heart as Face

Our hearts know intuitively divine truth while our minds can only find reason through discursive knowledge and cannot function properly except through the guidance of the higher intellect of our hearts. Our heart and our mind must work together to determine truth.

Awakening occurs in the heart not in the mind. The phrase "face and heart," carries a complex metaphoric meaning based on the conception of the beating heart as the symbol of the dynamic center of the person, and the face (not simply the physical face visible to others) as expressive of being in the deepest sense. The physical face, therefore, has the metaphoric potential to signify one's true face by manifesting those characteristics that make us "whole," that is, unique and well-integrated, as a result of the transformative process by which the outer appearance comes to reflect the inner, spiritual being. When this integration had been achieved, a person was said to have a "deified heart" and to be "master of himself."

Know Thyself is Not: Opinion of oneself, influenced by "first attention"[103] woundings. This leads to being unauthentic, pretending to be something that you are not: a false face. We need to replace our false face with our heart and develop our innate spiritual potential by becoming "one who divines things with their heart," one who infuses ordinary experience with spiritual energy. In other words, we need to understand our essentially spiritual nature and express it in the world of space and time—transforming the material world into spirit.[104]

Be Thyself – Be Authentic

It would be better for me if multitudes of men disagreed with me rather than that I, in the singleness of myself, should be out of harmony with myself
—Plato

Most importantly in "know thyself" is "be thyself – be authentic." One of the key ingredients of a happy, vibrant life is authenticity. When you live authentically – in line with your true self – you can focus your time and energy on what brings you the most joy. In other words, follow your true nature and be honest with yourself. It is the acceptance of one's self. Understand that each of us has a divine spark/fire within us but we are also each a unique human being. We each have an intrinsic aspect of self and soul. Do not fool yourself; be your own person; do not try to be someone or something else. This causes disharmony within the self and soul.

"Know thyself" is a warning applied to those whose boasts, and claims exceed who and what they are: "A person who is not themselves is a person lost from within. They have lost themselves by pretending to be someone/something else. Whatever the reasons may be for this deviation (stupidity, ignorance, fear, etc.) we can never attain inner bliss (eudaemonia) and wisdom when removed from our natural state of being - just as a tree cannot grow to its full potential when planted in unsuitable soil."[105]

One tragic reason for not being authentic is the prejudice of others showcased when you love someone of the same sex. And metaphorically, "stay in the closet." If this is the case say, "f_ _ k" you to them" and be who you are—the true and loving authentic self.

Bottom line: take care of yourself by knowing yourself and being yourself. Especially during this pandemic as we each need to take care of ourselves and keep strong and healthy: physically, mentally, and spiritually.

Know Thyself as a Mythic Hero

Myths are clues to the spiritual potentialities of the human life.[106]

A mythic hero is an individual, male or female, who ventures into the unknown where others dare not to go. It is through their heroic actions that the world becomes a better place. According to esteemed mythologist, Joseph Campbell, "The hero starts in the ordinary world, and receives a call to enter an unusual world of strange powers and events (a *call to adventure*). If the hero accepts the call to enter this strange world, the hero must face tasks and trials (a *road of trials*), and may have to face these trials alone, or may have assistance. At its most intense, the hero must survive a severe challenge, often with help earned along the journey. If the hero survives, the hero may achieve a great gift (the *goal* or *'boon'*), which often results in the discovery of important self-knowledge. The hero must then decide whether to return with this boon (the *return to the ordinary world*), often facing challenges on the return journey. If the hero is successful in returning, the boon or gift may be used to improve the world (the *application of the boon*)."[107]

In our own right each of us are heroes if we choose to accept the *call to adventure*. The adventure is the quest to awaken. This adventure is the great inner quest of "self." It is a heroic journey of knowing ourselves and our relationship to self and other. There are many obstacles to overcome. *Death must be confronted.* This is the death of the old self; our old consciousness, and with it, our second birth, our new consciousness. "In essence a hero's journey is towards transformation. And at the very end of that road, the transformation is likely to be a radical change of consciousness. Heroes and heroines are those who give their lives to something bigger than themselves. But this can transpire only when the hero is no longer identified with the ego[108]. Only then can there be a truly heroic transformation of consciousness.

The adventure to awaken has been mythically taught, though hidden, through various legends such as the Twelve Labors of the Greek hero Herakles, Óðinn's self-sacrifice and sacrifice self-to-self on the Norse World Tree, the Quest for the Golden Fleece and the Quest for the Holy Grail.

Our adventure, our inner quest is an inner struggle; the spiritual "struggle" within, that all people face—the conflict against our inner demons, past wounding's, and dysfunctional behaviors that no longer serve us, others, or the greater wellbeing. Add to this the stress and struggle of the pandemic. But without struggle, there is no progress.

This is the principle of transformation; an inward struggle of spiritually growth, doing right action and movement/change in life. Our lives are not meant to be static as in no evolution or transformation. Begin the journey; Become the hero of this pandemic—Quest. In this quest of knowing yourself, write the myth of your life and who you are as a mythic hero.

Do Far Travel

Sher with a serpent, Mexico

Far traveling, wandering to distant lands into the unknown, is necessary for awakening and spiritual power. A far traveler begins and then knows spirit of place. In other words, a far traveler is a spiritual pilgrim ever seeking the mysterium tremendum, the awe-inspiring mystery of the unknown. The blood-pulsing passion of life is found at the edge of the unknown. Far traveling is not vacation. It is not traveling to a place just because it is the "in thing," as it is to go to Iceland, and years ago, sadly, Machu Picchu. A far traveler goes on holiday, or holy day, and is not a tourist but an adventurer, a pilgrim of spirit on a journey of self-knowledge. Pilgrimage means going out and finding something. And that something equates to many things: our true self, compassion, love of self and nature, and accepting and understanding our self and others not like us. In other words, you will learn about yourself and others not like you. And this will grow your compassion and empathy.

In forty years of far traveling, Sher and I have experienced things that seen mythic and the story line from an Indian Jones adventure movie: my vision of the star and hearing the voice from heaven; the blazing red eyes of a long-dead monk; gigantic pillars of light—angels— and glowing gigantic green rocks that grew from small ones; spirit encounters on the battlements of an old Welsh castle, and with an awakened dragon-spirit in a Cornish cave; spirit dancing in the smoke- houses of British Columbia; downing bottles of posh (cane alcohol or what I call shamanic white lightning) in a night-long ceremony in the highlands of Mexico with a *Zinacantec* (Bat) shaman; receiving a message from a spirit-man at midnight outside the sacred city of Teotihuacán; being clawed by a jaguar shape-shifter under a pyramid in the Yucatan jungles; knowing Oneness after a descending spirit exorcism at midnight in front of a mausoleum on the sacred mountain of K yasan, Japan; chased by killer bees after almost dying—my death initiation—on a mountain peak in Peru; a hungry Hawaiian spirit, the flying meatloaf; a long-dead Northwest Coast sea serpent; a Japanese succubus; the gate-keeping dwarf of Machu Picchu; the "hidden ones" of Iceland; the Yakuza and the wounded vet, and so many other expe- riences. These tales are told within our memoirs. After this pandemic is under control, please consider far traveling outside of this country.

Life is School

The native Hawaiians believed that life was school. And they still see life as a school where learning takes place as long as they lived. The Hawaiian way was to believe that we had been born to learn, and we would continue to learn as long as we walked the earth. Children's teachers were members of their own family. Who could better know their needs?[109]

As we can see this is not our present educational philosophy, which I believe is a determent to our children. Testing seems to be the only concern. How about you? If you have a child/children are you teaching them about life? Or are you leaving it totally in the hands of others? We all understand that school is important. Safely returning children to school is essential. The "key" word here is safely. And the tragedy here is that there is not a national plan to safely open our schools.

* * *

This pandemic is an excellent time to ponder your life's journey and journal about it. Have you seen your life as a lifelong adventure of learning? Or has it been about consuming things and making money as being more important than learning new information and knowledge about other things and yourself—self-knowledge?

After pondering this and your life's journey, journal about your life during this pandemic. After various periods of time, ponder and write about what you have learned about yourself and others during this pandemic.

* * *

Concerning your life's journey, put part of your focus on the time or times when you made a major life decision. What came from that decision and what would have been the alternative path in your life? For instance, did you take a job or entered a profession because of money or pressure from others, such as parents? Did you marry someone not for love, but for family reasons, money, prestige, and/or security? Be honest with yourself.

The most pivotal point in our life and the decision that came from it occurred on a sacred mountaintop in Japan in 1987:

While I jetted off to Japan on a spiritual and warrior pilgrimage known as a *musha shugyo*, my wife was back in Maine preparing our home to be sold. Three years prior, my father had passed over at a very young age. He was only fifty-eight and had built over many years a successful small business. Being the only child, my mother was lonely and kept reminding me that I was the only child. Continuously, since my father had passed over, she had been pressuring my wife and I to "come back home" and take over the business.

Ah, she was using society's rules: be responsible, make lots of money, work for works sake and the lure of retirement – the Great American Dream. And all wrapped up in a pretty package of guilt. Ironically, guilt[110] is usually not a button pusher for me. But still, my wife and I decided to move back to our hometown in Maryland and take over the business. The United States Senate was one of my wellness clients and I rationalized that I would be closer and wouldn't have to travel all the way from Maine to Washington D.C.

But then again, guilt is not one of my rules of life, nor is money for retirement. The magic of K yasan—the joy of its peacefulness and its power of nature, this sacred mountain and my own innate spiritual, philosophical and esoteric self—led me to another realization and a life changing decision. Did this realization come in a vision or a dream? Far from it; it came in my everyday present moment of wakefulness as – I know things. And the decision: we were not moving.[111]

Divine Human Exercise

The focus of your mind determines your reality and the quality of your heart. Therefore, instead of focusing on the negative human-ness of yourself and life (the pandemic, criticism, fear, anger, revenge, etc.) focus on the divineness of yourself and life (love, beauty, light, praise, loved ones, etc.). Pick a day to begin—then in the morning, look into a mirror, into your eyes, see not the past or your negative humanness, but the present—your divinity. During the day focus on the present as a divine human. Spend some time alone out in nature and focus on the beauty and the love of nature in all its grandeur; the sun, the clouds, the birds, animals, trees, flowers, etc. At the end of the day, observe the divinity of a sunset and during the night, the wonder and awe of the moon and the stars. Sleep in peace and arise at first light and greet the dawn, its beauty and divinity and realize that this divinity has always been there for you. As this new day dawns, I would ask that you begin to balance your divinity and your humanity in this awesome journey that we call life.

2. ACCEPT THE POWER WITHIN

During and after this pandemic, it is important for our health of heart and mind to understand—"we have power." True power is within us. We are able to be courageous and conduct the changes and transformations that are needed. Be responsible, wear a mask; it expresses your inner power, compassion, and loving kindness to others—love others as thyself. Have a caring and compassionate attitude for others. Would you want your child or elder/parent to suffer and possibly die due to your arrogance and uncaring nature?

Even though we have a spark of God, the divine fire within us, our human self will make mistakes. Not wearing a mask is not a mistake, but a unprincipled selfish act, one that is uncaring, stupid, and arrogant.

We don't have to be stupid and arrogant—instead we can awaken our divine fire within us. In other words, if we accept the belief that we are divine as well as human, then, logically, we have the power within us to transform, to forgive, to be compassionate, to embrace and express loving kindness and divine unconditional love, to feel at peace, and to feel togetherness not separateness. It is possible to awaken, due to the starry heavenly vibrational divine essence that is our true heart, our true self, and our true soul.

* * *

Our minds constantly seek power. The key factor is what do we consider power to be? If our focus is on self, the "I," the "me," our sense of power will be externally based on the currently acceptable social and cultural paradigms that deem the person powerful and successful. In the case of Americans, this would include, but not limited to, the capitalistic driven Great American Dream and the so-called Protestant work ethic of work, work, work. It is in this scenario where mental freedom evaporates into an unmanageable mix of stress and success. As the head takes the heart where it possibly does not want to go.

On the contrary, when we experience reality based on our power being within or internally sourced from our divineness and humanness and our self as an interpenetrating oneness of the "I" and the "we," freedom of the mind and heart are re-established resulting in an authentic state of being—who we truly are. When we establish an authenticity of self as a divine human being with our heart and mind as one, we begin walking a path of love, peace, and harmony.

We are, in fact, never alone. We are connected to everything on this earth. If we can stretch our imagination, we are connected to every star and galaxy in creation. Our star essence of light within us is as important to God (the One, Great Mystery, the All) as the grandest galaxy. One cannot exist without the other—please ponder this concept.

* * *

We have the power to live in peace and to be in harmony—to generate inner peace within our mind and body. We have to power to destroy the passions[112] of our mind—to be at peace with ourselves and others. Let us walk gently and be in peace as we journey through life.

This power within us may be symbolically termed our Holy Grail—the sacred cup that contains our star essence. It is our heart that is the sacred reservoir of our holy blood, and it is in that moment between heartbeats, that our creative transformation takes place. We may be viewed as co-creators but on the other hand, we are really transformers in an ecstatic dance of cosmic proportions. We are each fallen angels striving to return home with "brighter wings." In our journey of awakening, our power is generated through self-control, present moment awareness, empathy, compassion, patience, perseverance, forgiveness, confidence, and sacrifice. What is the power of our Holy

Grail—Love. As the Grail can only be attained by love, not striving, and our heart will become pure spirit—of love, freedom, and happiness.

Sacrifice

The Hot Gates of Thermopylae – Late August 480 B.C.E.

"Our army is great," the Persian says, "and because
of the number of our arrows you will not see the sky!"
Then a Spartan answers: "In the shade, therefore, we will fight!"
And Leonidas, king of the Spartans, shouts: "Fight with spirit
Spartans; perhaps we will dine today among the ghosts!"
– Cicero

In the annals of heroic action and sacrifice the Greek stand at the pass of Thermopylae echoes down through eternity and show-cases qualities we all need to embrace during and after this pandemic especially sacrifice: loyalty, courage, honor, vigilance, perseverance and fortitude, struggle, bravery, and heroic action. Spartan King Leonidas, 60 years of age at Thermopylae, his 300 Spartan hoplites and approximately 6700 other Greeks stood against a Persian land army numbering around 360,000—400,000 combatants. The ancient Greek historian, Herodotus, simply states the "holding action" of the Spartans and other Greeks in an epitaph:

Oh, stranger, tell the Lacedaemonians that here
we lie dead, obedient to their commands.

2020 marks the 2500th Anniversary of the Greek action and sacrifice at Thermopylae. I know in my heart and soul Thermopylae. To celebrate my 60th birthday in 2006, I walked the battlefield, known today as the Hot Gates. From our memoirs:

Before setting foot on the battleground, I removed my shoes and walked barefoot across the sacred and hallowed ground of Thermopylae. My family knew to leave me alone with my thoughts and memories. The sparsely treed ground was hard and scorching as if that time almost 2,500 years ago was imbedded forever in the cracked Earth beneath my feet.

Walking as if in a trance, I could smell why this sacred ground was known as the Hot Gates. In front of me were the purified waters of the flowing, volcanic sulphurous springs. As an act of purification, remembrance, and personal penance, I dipped my feet into their indescribably hot waters. I endured the pain that I felt I needed to feel as a tear slowly slid down my cheek. The searing waters and the rocky ground mirrored to me their witness and my soul's knowing of that heroic battle...

The Spartans and the other Greek hoplites gave the ultimate sacrifice. Down through the ages many others have also given the ultimate sacrifice. In the present day, essential workers are sacrificing. Isn't it a small price and sacrifice for you and others to wear a mask and social distance? Do you have the courage, compassion, and empathy to do so?

Confidence

Nothing is as universal as stupidity
—Cicero

During this pandemic do not accept the view of others, the ones who spread doubt, false views, and attachment. Simply put, this is doubting the truth of science and medical experts, believing the false view and narrative that the virus is not real while embracing conspiracy theories, and the attachment to the past—the so-called normal.

Instead, adopt confidence and follow the advice of medical authorities. This is extremely important to the health of our heart, mind, and spirit. Confidence occurs from accepting ourselves — from knowing who we are and accepting ourselves. If we accept the power that resides within us, then through self-confidence, without the presence of doubt (whether hidden or conscious), anything is possible.

In other words, we need to release the doubts that we harbor. But where does our doubt lurk hidden away? Pure and simple, it exists in our fear. Fear breeds uncertainty and doubt. The more that we doubt ourselves and doubt others, our life becomes a world of shadows where we see humanity not as love but as fear. This depressing cloud of doubt hanging over our head transforms our life into a dark existence of uncertainty and inaction. When we doubt, we don't Do; we may exist but without the vitality of living. It becomes far too easy to make excuses for the lack of doing and put the responsibility for our life on the shoulders of others. Steeped in doubt, we lack faith—faith in ourselves, faith in others and faith in the loving creation of life.[113]

How can we stay on the surface of the sea of life and not let doubt, fear, and the other debilitating and incapacitating emotions overcome us? Learn to walk on water.

Walking on Water

The Book of Matthew (14:24-31) describes how the disciples, particularly Peter, yearn to walk on the unruly, wind-tossed seas of life, just as Jesus does. Shortly before dawn, Peter is commanded to simply get out of the little boat and start walking on the water. He begins securely enough, but immediately, thinking about the dangers, and glancing down at the black waters… "he became afraid, and beginning to sink, he cried out…'Lord, save me!'" Jesus replied, "O you of little faith,[114] why did you doubt?"

This story is metaphoric and hides important teachings. One clue is "shortly before dawn." This is the transitional transformative time between the dark of night and the light of day. This is the time frame when I bathe and bathe others. It has been documented that after Jesus' experience of the descending spirit of the dove while bathing conducted by John-the-Baptist, Jesus was given the power to begin bathing others—a transformative process of death and rebirth, a second birth while still alive.

The second most important teaching is the act of walking on water which represents the miraculous ability of Jesus to detach from emotional states (the rough water) and thus, not sink into the deep waters of fear, doubt, and anger. Instead of sinking or drowning in the rough waters of life, we have the ability to release and detach from the materialistic dependent life—a source of our rough waters. This teaching message reminds us to have faith in all circumstances—confidence in the divine light that is within each of us and within all of creation. At this time of the "Great Struggle," we each need faith and love to keep us "walking on the unruly sea of life."

* * *

In the biblical story related above, Peter's intent is to walk on water. He knows it is possible because he has witnessed (metaphorically)

Jesus walking on the waves. However, when Peter tries it, fear creeps in, doubt surfaces, and he loses his focus. He forgets his intent, throws away his confidence, and starts to sink. In our human journey, we sometimes tend to "sink" instead of walking on the waves of life.

It is so easy for us to lose our will, intent, and our focus. This allows doubt, fear, and uncertainty to creep into our consciousness, especially during this pandemic. This leads to a sense of powerlessness and a lack of love and trust in us and in others. The uncertainty of life only further reinforces this doubt of ourselves. This leads us to view reality through the prism of fear and separation. Our uncertainty keeps us frozen in the past and a fearful future where no true happiness, love, and compassion can occur in the present.

How do we break out of this prism of fear and separation? The answer, pure and simple, is through our expression of love. By conveying our deep love, we can begin to harmonize our lives and thus find that jewel of happiness that is our life's journey. With this light of love as our guide, we learn to trust in life and to believe and to understand that everything in life works out for the best, maybe not what we expected, but what is truly best for the evolution of our soul. To help guide us in awakening, we need to believe not only in ourselves, but also in the sacredness of nature and all things of the earth.

Power of Sound

The mysteries of life are amazing as witnessed by our initial sound of power. It is not our birth cry. It is not the first sound that we make on earth. Our first sound is the sound of divine breath (our soul) entering our mortal body. It was known to the ancient religious philosophers as H — "the creative word, the seed of fire, the first sound."[115] It was the Greek E[116] of creation, the Hebrew E (Hé) [117] of breath – soul, and the E of Einstein's formula. We may look at $H\bar{u}$ as the sound of the

Sixth Element or Cosmic Consciousness. Connected with *Hū* is the powerful seed-syllable *Hūm*, symbolized by a flame or flaming drop.

Certain words or sounds may be considered "seed syllables." A seed syllable is one sound that contains the whole essence of one thing. Seeds portray the vibrational imagery of life unseen. From the primal explosion of a seed comes the potential within. Or is it the reality within? Existence, growth, and then, is it death, or back to the seed?

And thus, it is so with the concept of the "seed syllable." A breath of power, a manifestation in form, all contained within the seed. A primal sound in structure but then again creative creation supreme. This is the secret of truth and light. But it is not to be grasped; only to be experienced with the heart. The mind struggles refusing to grant this heightened knowledge and only desiring the tangible form that in its seeking of its own egocentric power says: reality is form and form is reality.

But, the heart knows the truth. The seed is the heart. The sound is the heart. This sound is *Hū/Hé* —male/female. *Hū* is the inhalation of our breath from the Absolute, un-originated world of the Great Mystery. While the exhalation of our breath is the Relative, originated world of creation—*Hé*.

One way to stay "sane" and relaxed during this pandemic is at various times during the day stop your mind chatter, stop worrying, and do the following breathing/vocalization: Inhale with mouth open an audible *Hū* (sounds like 'you') and exhale with an audible *Hé* (sounds like 'hay'). Repeat as appropriate. Be careful in the beginning, as this experience will make you breathe deeper than normal and may cause dizziness.

Hū being a seed syllable may be utilized to increase one's spirit power. There are two sounds that may be chanted: one being *Hū* with a 'you' sound and the second with a 'who' sound. In addition, to empower our throat chakra (energy swirl), which will affect the power of our speech, we may chant *Hū* with our lips almost closed producing a sound like the buzzing of bees or a powerboat sound.

AHAVAH—LOVE

As I mentioned before, *Ahavah* means "love" in Hebrew. And there is a connection between the word *ahavah*, "love," and *"echad*," one. The numerical value of their letters is the same: 13. Interesting to note that within the word, *Ahavah*, resides an esoteric Buddhism "seed" syllable *vah* meaning Entry into Nirvāna.

Vowel sounds are powerful and transformative. Vowels vibrate, linger, and endure. Their energetic power vibrates within the cells and essence of our body. Let love vibrate within us by chanting *Ahavah*: *A (au) ha vah* while visualizing a divine seed of light or spark within our heart. And what to do with your hands: in a comfortable seated position put the back of your right hand on the palm of your left hand (both facing to the sky) at the level of your belly button with thumbs lightly touching symbolizing a small flame and slowly chant repeatedly *A (au) ha vah* (see position below).

Meditating while sitting on Intihuatana, Hitching Post of the Sun, Machu Picchu, 1988 with my hands in the meditation mudra— Jō-in Mudra. It is made by taking the open left hand palm up and placed on the lap and then placing the open

right hand palm up over it with the two thumbs touching pointing upwards. The five fingers of the right hand symbolize the five Elements of the Divine World and the five fingers of the left hand symbolize the five Elements of world of sentient beings. The thumbs represent the Element of Space. This mudra represents the non-duality of all beings and the Divine.

OM—AUM

The most recognizable power word or sound is OM or AUM. The sound of this word "represents to our ears that sound of the energy of the universe of which all things are manifestations. You start in the back of the mouth 'ahh,' and then 'oo,' you fill the mouth, and 'mm,' closes the mouth. When you pronounce this properly, all vowel sounds are included in the pronunciation. AUM. Consonants are here regarded simply as interruptions of the essential vowel sound.

"A-U-M. The birth, the coming into being, and the dissolution that cycles back. AUM is called the 'four-element syllable.' A-U-M—and what is the fourth element? The silence out of which AUM arises, and back into which it goes, and which underlies it, too."[118]

The Fullness of the Primordial Night

The ancient Hawaiians utilized the power of vocalization and breath through the magic of chant. Even to the point of chanting vowels as a religious breathing exercise from their creation myth *Kumulipo*: *O pihā ū, o pihā ā, o pihā ē, o pihā ō* - Full of u, full of a, full of e, full of o. The breath was connected to the environment. The chanter would imitate the winds. Breath was connected to the insides of a person and could impart his or her power. The breath carried the word and added to its own intrinsic hum.[119]

Eternal Parent—The One

O'ono is a short repetitive Hawaiian chant. A most powerful chant is a greeting to the *Eternal Parent,* (The One), *the ever expanding vine: AUMAKUA MAULOA, E lei, ie, ie, ie, ie, ie, ie, ie, ie.*[120] Be focused with a strong mind and intent, chant eight times, draw out and hold the sound of the last vowels. *AUUU MAAA KUUU AAAA MAUU LOOO AAAA - E lei, ie, ie, ie, ie, ie, ie, ie, ie.* When complete, maintain being centered with a strong mind in silence for a self-determined period of time. Record any feelings or insights.

Silence

Only when thou drunkest from the rivers of silence wilt thou learn to sing.[121]

Silence is golden as the saying goes. Ironically enough, for most people silence is an unknown quality, in fact something to be shunned. The more external chatter and internal mind talk the less opportunity to come face to face with our true authentic selves. This chatter prevents us from facing our imperfections and wounding's that may be unveiled to us when we are silent. What our incessant talk and mind chatter only accomplishes is pure and simple, stupidity which holds the seeds of ignorance, arrogance, and greed.

The divine and mundane interpenetrate. What this means is that the quieter the mind and tongue, the more we can hear nature and nature's divine voice. If we desire to speak to trees, we must first listen to them. One of the key teachings of the Northwest Coast First People as well as other indigenous cultures is the refrain to listen, look, and learn. Begin now during this pandemic to remember that silence (quiet mind and no idle chatter) is golden. Silence may open us to stillness of mind and spirit. It is one of the secrets to our power within and the power of our words and sounds.

Chakras

The common meaning of chakra is an energy vortex. That would be correct if we are talking about the exoteric meaning. But what many do not know is the original esoteric meaning. The original name meant "discus," as in the lethal throwing weapon, with the meaning of destroying the passions that hinder a person's journey towards enlightenment. Passions mean anything that disrupts the tranquility of the mind. This meaning implies the esoteric importance of our body's energy centers or chakras.

Additionally, chakras are depositories of memory. Our emotional wounding's and the past issues connected with those wounding's may be locked away within the various chakras. These blockages will affect and inhibit the energy flow throughout our body. Over time this disharmony will affect the body's various health systems such as the organs and glands. There are seven chakras; below is a brief description of the first chakra.

❖ Root Chakra: It is located at the base of the spine and deals with issues of security, basic needs, and basic human survival. It also deals with issues of profane sex, inappropriate sexual activity, and one's sense of "roots" and family and their connection to the earth (an un-awakened first chakra views earth/nature as hostile). Our connection to family is rooted in our connection to ancestors. And our ancestors are intertwined and connected with the sacredness of the earth.

This is the chakra of dualism and fear. Endocrine System: Reproductive Glands/Adrenals. Color symbolism is red. Earth Element. This chakra represents Plutonian energy. Ruled by Saturn.

Fear

Do Not Take Counsel of Your Fears
—General Stonewall Jackson

Do not permit fear and uncertainty to determine your course in life. Fear is a reality of human existence. In a few instances it may help us in life by waking us out of a complacent stupor. Furthermore, our "fight and/or flight" mechanism helps us deal effectively with fear. The ones connected with any life and death situation. But there is another category of fear. This fear is by far, the most damaging to us. It is our worst enemy. It is insidious. Daily, it steals a part of our soul. It is the fear that separates—the fear of the unknown. This is the pandemic.

The first recourse to help deal with our fear is for each of us to appreciate life and what we have, not what we do not have. Next accept the fragile and frailness of life while accepting the sacrifice of others for our safety and wellbeing—essential workers. The frontline workers and first responders sacrifice their own health and safety for us. The nurses, doctors, all hospital workers, firemen/women, police, teachers, and many others such as truckers and garbage collectors putting their lives on the line for us. When the "clarion horn" was blown, the call to action, they did not run the other way but answered it in a selfless manner. Many times, the blowing of the horn falls to the hero—no doubt, they are heroes. Be thankful, and bless them all.

Fear slowly eats away at the core of our heart.
—JC

The fear of the unknown is the fear of death, but also, the fear of life, which creates a sense of powerlessness within us. With this virus we need to understand the long-term effects of it on our life, which are not pretty such as fatigue and difficulty concentrating or focusing. Studies have found that the disease may cause myocarditis, inflammation of the heart muscle, also damage the brain. "COVID-19, the disease caused by the new coronavirus, is largely a respiratory illness that affects the lungs, but neuroscientists and specialist brain doctors say emerging evidence of its impact on the brain is concerning. If in a year's time we have 10 million recovered people, and those people have cognitive deficits ... then that is going to affect their ability to work and their ability to go about activities of daily living."[122]

We cannot be shut away forever. In the meantime, be considerate and smart. When venturing out, we need to be considerate of others and our own self by social distancing and wearing a mask.

* * *

Fear has been increasing and the ramping-up since the appearance of the coronavirus. To think not is foolish. Fear in some circumstances is beneficial as long as it does not inhibit or impede us from doing what is necessary—necessary is the key word, be disciplined. Anyone entering combat without fear is lying to themselves. The fear is pressed down so that it does not affect you or you brothers and sisters in arms. Then hopefully after the conflict, the suppressed fear is brought to the surface and purged.

Presently, our fears are numerous and in front of our consciousness where in pre-pandemic times they were usually in the back of our minds. This is the fear of ourselves and loved ones dying and/or getting sick and sometimes, extremely sick. It is the fear for the safety and wellbeing of family and friends. It is the fear for our children and their teachers going back to school and staying in school—a perfect petri dish. Children and their teachers are more important than money and opening the economy. Children are precious—money is not.

Fear is the opposite of love. One antidote to help with our fear is to express love. Use every chance to speak your love to others, to family, extended family, and friends.

* * *

Fear will keep us from our bliss and an awakened heart. We must access the inner core of our strength—our heart, which will help us bring our fears out of the darkness and into the light. This transformational power, we all have within us. It fosters the courage for us to face fear. Confronting our fears, we are then able to let go of some, transform others, and finally make peace with the fears that we cannot let go of or transform. It is normal and human to be afraid, just never let it inhibit your life or keep you from your bliss. To conquer fear is to triumph over death. So, what fears do you still harbor? Which ones can be released? The ones not released, which ones can be detached from or "pressed down"?

To help us get through this pandemic we need to work with our first chakra issues. As we transmute these issues from being based on fear to being based on interconnectedness and love, we come closer to happiness—even with the virus hanging over our heads. We have the power to achieve our own world of peace and harmony—we have the power to achieve what others only fantasize about.

During this coronavirus, we need unity not divisiveness. Even with the fear of the virus, we have entered into an even more dangerous period of time, with the long-term effects—not known. This country is divided, and it does not help this acrimony that the planet Mars on June 27th entered the constellation of Ares (god of war). Mars relates to a person's basic instincts representing energy, aggression, desire, competition, and the sex drive. "Mars transiting through its own sign of Aries is extremely dynamic and will dominate the second half of 2020, especially during the retrograde phase from September 9 to November 13. Mars will also be conjunct Eris, Goddess of Discord, for the second half of 2020 (exact in August, October, and December). It cannot escape our notice that this Mars retrograde period coincides with the United States presidential election on November 3. Mars retrograde can 'fight dirty,' so this may portend a particularly combative election campaign, with anger and divisiveness continuing after the election is over. When Mars begins retrograde, we may feel particularly reactive and, therefore, be easily triggered, so we all need to watch for that."[123] This points out the important point that each of us has the potential to commit horrendous dreadful acts of violence. This violence is connected with our primal beastly nature. By overcoming the dark passions such as fear and revenge, the hero symbolizes our ability to control the irrational savage (beast) within us.

He whose mind is enslaved to his bestial instincts is philosophically not superior to the brute, he whose rational faculties ponder human affairs is a man; and he whose intellect is elevated to the consideration of divine realities is already a demigod, for his being partakes of the luminosity with which his reason has brought him into proximity.[124]

The Beast Within

Jesus said: Blessed is the lion which the man eats, and the lion will become man; and cursed is the man whom the lion eats, and the lion will become man.[125]

There is an ancient cross-cultural concept referred to as "the beast within." The beast commonly portrayed as a lion, a jaguar, or a wolf. It symbolizes the untamed nature of our primitive (reptilian and paleomammalian) or hindbrain where instincts such as survival, dominance, and mating are located. Metaphorically then, our beast is an inner quality that is intimately connected with our first chakra issues of safety, security, survival, and sex. All humans have a fierceness and ferociousness within themselves—the beast within.[126] Consciously, many people ignore this quality of self; many fear it, while others deny it totally. But our inner beast is neutral. It is not, by its nature, solely a positive (constructive) or a negative (destructive) quality. Think of our beast as the totality of our strength, will power, and sexual potency. These are also important qualities which we need in our lives in order to be fully human, fully healthy, and fully energetic.

However, these qualities, and others, may be turned negative or destructive through such emotions as: denial, madness, anger, extreme anger or rage, substance abuse, revenge, envy, hate, jealousy, and fear.[127] Add to this list, the issues of power, greed, and control over others— seem familiar. It is easy to see the potential of unleashing the dysfunctional and destructive dark qualities of our beast.

Too often we forget that without the dark, there would be no light. Our lives are usually organized into a separation between the symbolic light and symbolic dark with the light held up as our ultimate goal in spiritual/religious life.[128] On the contrary, brilliance needs darkness in order to be appreciated to its full extent.[129]

The true secret that most never realize is that light and dark are equal components within us that interpenetrate as one reality. True spiritual/religious teachings are then based on the acknowledgement of this interpenetrative aspect of dark and light and then the growth of our light or the divine aspect of our soul from the creative darkness of our humanity.

This is not the Jungian concept of the "shadow," but the actual and physical reality of dualistic concepts such as light and dark, spirit and matter, which interpenetrate. The dualistic separation of light and dark are the illusion as our individual sense of reality is an extension of the illusion of our basic core sense perceptions. Our eyes perceive separation between us, and all things viewed (as one of our senses, the eyes are overrated). This constant reinforcement tricks us in to thinking and believing that we are separate and an island unto ourselves. The reality is that we are not separate at all but deeply interconnected as we have discovered during this pandemic.

Do not fear the dark, only be afraid of what is hidden in the dark.

As we discovered, our symbolic light and dark blend together within us, which defines our wholeness as an individual. Furthermore, there are two sides to our inner darkness. There is no separate shadow just a darkness that is both creative and destructive at the same time.

The "shadow" is considered an archetype by Jungians[130] and connected with the unconscious but Jung advanced no connection to physiological reality. With the concept of the dark, there is a connection to the body—testosterone. This hormone is our bodily source of physical strength, will power, and sexual potency. Testosterone is the source of our beast within.

This important hormone is made in large amounts by the testicles of men. But testosterone is not limited solely to men. Women produce testosterone in their ovaries even though it is only about one tenth of what a male produces just as a male produces a small amount of the female hormone estrogen. Additionally, both men and women produce a small amount of testosterone in their adrenal glands which are the source of our fight/flight mechanism—the power of our beast. But, "the modern, technological world gives us few positive outlets for this energy, and yet the pressures of our lives are constantly causing our bodies to send us hormonal messages to fight or flee."[131]

* * *

It is the beast within ignored or turned negative which is the root cause of the seemingly ever-present physical (including excessive force by police), sexual, and mental abuse issues found within all levels and stratums of society. There is another major issue. The untamed beast is literally stupidity and ignorance running rampant. Ignorance, not to be equated with educational level or one's intelligence, along with stupidity are both rooted in a materialistic dualistic view of life. This results in a spiritually un-awakened consciousness.

This ignorance then inflates and protects the unhealthy ego's sense of self-survival resulting in arrogance and arrogant behavior. In turn, this arrogance feeds the untamed beast. This is the very same arrogance that turns a blind eye or denial to all forms of abuse, such as sexual abuse especially if reporting or stopping the abuse would threaten the person's external power and/or position in the world. Sadly, there are too many examples to list.

* * *

The beast wants to constantly feed its source of power.[132] There is even a term and title for the most ravenous and power hungry— lionized. Sounds very familiar. The beast is the source of dysfunctional sexual behavior. This is not sexual issues the church rules as dysfunctional such as homosexuality, but the sexual dysfunction that harms another individual such as pedophilia, rape, and incest. It can also manifest in the manipulation of another for power, control, or influence.

It is important to understand; the beast lies within each of us, male and female alike. As much as we may want to deny our beast within, doing so would be denying our own source of physical strength and potency. Our denial of the dark leaves our light in a vulnerable position in its so-called sole existence of truth. The dark is symbolic of our creative potentiality. A quality we would not want to destroy or inhibit. Additionally, denial may lead to a consciousness of passive victimization. Metaphorically, our "sword arm" is impotent and figuratively "cut off."

Denying the beast within may allow it de facto permission to run wild. The Roman Catholic Church and other institutions are guilty of this denial. Look at how the Church's denial has manifested into the world - vulnerable children abused. But to shift the blame, the Church provides a substitute for the beast in the guise of the Devil—the Devil made me do it. In an interview the previous Pope Benedict "acknowledged some of the church's failings, like in the sexual-abuse crisis, which he called 'a volcano of filth' sent by the devil."[133]

Titans

There is an interesting myth on why the beast is within us. According to the ancient Greek Mystery Religion of Orphism the beast came to be found within every human being as a result of a conflict between Zeus and the Titans:

> The Orphics taught that the god Dionysus, as a child, had been slain by the evil Titans. One day, while innocently playing with some toys—dice, a top, a ball, a mirror, apples, a bull-roarer, and a tuft of wool—the Titans approached Dionysus from behind. They ripped him to shreds[134] and devoured his fragments. Infuriated at the senseless attack, Zeus destroyed the Titans with his thunderbolt. From the ashes of the Titans humanity came into being. Because humanity arose from the ashes of the Titans, people possess a lawless and sometimes destructive "Titanic" nature. However, because the Titans had consumed Dionysus, humanity also contains a Divine Spark of Dionysus. This is the essential Self, a spark of the Godhead, which possesses eternal life.[135]

According to the Orphics, "The world is pictured as a Wheel, the ever-spinning realm of generation, the cycle of incarnations. Through asceticism and spiritual practice, it is possible to help purify the soul of its Titanic nature and strengthen the Divine Spark within. Then, if we attain a sufficient level of spiritual realization, it is possible eventually to transcend the cycle of births and deaths and live eternally with the gods."[136]

In our journey of awakening, we must "slay" our beast through the process of transmutation. In other words, tame and awaken our beast within. This will transform it into an inner quality of altruistic strength, divine will power, and altruistic sexual potency—love as profane and sacred sexuality. These are the qualities that are based on love, not on fear, control, manipulation, or revenge. We still possess the power of the beast, but it is tamed and will work for our benefit and the benefit of the earth and humanity. This is the strength and power to awaken our inner spark, achieve Divinehood while defending the downtrodden. No longer do we express excessive aggression; no longer do we have the impulse or need to abuse or destroy other people or other things.

Redemption

This lesson of overcoming the beast within has been taught down through the ages through myth and legend for thousands of years. It is a lesson of redemption as it concerns the hero who has transgressed, caused pain to others and done un-noble, sometimes horrific, acts and behaviors. The best-known myth comes from Greece and depicts the life and times of the hero Herakles.

Herakles was born in Thebes and was the son of Alcmene and Amphitryon. Even though Herakles father was Amphitryon he was on the other hand sired by Zeus i.e. he was divine as well as human. Herakles life story unfolds as a metaphoric teaching of self-redemption from separateness to awakening and ultimate oneness symbolized by his twelve labors climaxing in his twelfth—The Capture of Cerberus.[137]

After completing each labor his essential divinity was further revealed to him as he approached Divinehood. Herakles began his quest for redemption only after he had committed the ultimate betrayal and beastly act. In a fit of madness, destructive anger, and rage, Herakles killed his wife and children. Realizing what he had done he retreated into the wilderness full of remorse and isolated himself. Only through the urging of his cousin Theseus did Herakles travel to Delphi to receive the advice of the Oracle. Thus, was born the twelve labors.

It is through the first labor that Herakles conquered his beast within symbolized by the slaying of the Nemean Lion. Of his twelve labors slaying the beast first, symbolic of taming his own beastly nature, allowed him to successfully complete the other eleven labors.

The lion was laying waste to the land transforming it from its essential paradise into a wasteland. The lion symbolizes constructive strength and power but also the destructive side of untamed nature. External physical weapons could not harm it or penetrate its impermeable skin. It was only the inner will, strength, power, and courage of Herakles that could overcome this beast. Herakles confronted the lion in its lair or cave, which had two openings. Herakles blocked one off and then entered the other fighting the beast with just his hands. This symbolized that Herakles power lies not in his weapons but in his hands.[138] A power that is internal, direct, and personal within each of us.

After a furious battle he finally succeeded in crushing the life out of it. Victorious Herakles knew that he needed to wear the skin of the beast that he had just overcome.[139]

This imagery demonstrates Herakles controlling the lion's body (symbolizing strength) and neutralizing the lion's tail (symbolizing power[140]).

An ordinary knife would not work on the impervious skin of the lion. Athena, the Greek goddess of wisdom, heroes, and intelligent courage, instructed Heracles how to remove the skin by using the lion's own claws. Thus, the lion's hide became Heracles' signature garment with the upper half of the lion's head sitting atop his head as a helmet. This lion's skin would become his symbol showing that he had conquered the beast. "And the lion becomes man."

There is a further clue to the meaning of Herakles overcoming the power and ferociousness of the lion. For this we turn to the mythic centaur symbolic of wisdom and the union of human and beast. Our focus is on one particular wise centaur, the half mortal-half divine— Chiron, who was the teacher of Herakles as well as Achilles, Orpheus, and Jason. Chiron was a master of medicine, music, gymnastics, warfare, and astrology, and the founder of the ancient healing temple *Asclepeion*. With his mastery and background, Chiron, half-horse/half-man, embraced and exemplified the warrior-healer.

Since the centaur symbolized human and beast united as one, the wise Chiron "represents complete integration of human and bestial vitality."[141] Both Herakles and Chiron reveal the teaching that there is no separation between the physical and spiritual, between us and the rest of creation.

Know thy Beast

The first step in awakening our divine spark is to know thyself. Denying the beast within is the polar opposite of this principle. When we know ourselves and recognize and accept our primal nature, we bring liberation and transformation to ourselves.

By examining Herakles beastly transgression and his first labor, we discover how this applies to our life and our journey of awakening. The power is within us to be either altruistic or selfish/self-seeking/ self-seeking. During the pandemic, many demonstrated this selfishness: "don't give a damn about others" by refusing to wear a mask and social distance. Many of these were professed Christians—their so-called freedom and liberty "trumped" following the teachings of Jesus (do unto others).

During this pandemic, we need to have the courage and inner strength of Herakles to face our own inner beast, so we can tame and awaken it—awaken our altruistic power. We achieve the strength and will power of the lion to be utilized as altruistic strength, divine will power, and altruistic sexual potency in our journey of awakening.

As Jesus taught in the Gospel of Thomas, the lion symbolizes our beast within representing the strength, courage, and vigor of our primitive self, but it can also be potentially savage, uncontrollable, destructive, and devouring of our empathic self. If the lion, the beast within, stays un-awakened (spiritually) - untamed (mentally, physically) there is the potential for our first chakra actions and behaviors to be dysfunctional and possibly abusive. This is the unhealthy ego seeing reality only from the "I" and the first chakra. In Jesus' words, the lion has eaten the man "and the lion will become man" and the man is cursed. However, if we awaken the altruistic power of the lion, we have symbolically eaten the lion instead of the lion eating us. We are blessed not cursed; "and the lion will become man." Being blessed is metaphorically the equivalent of achieving the healthy ego where reality is based on the "I or me" in the "we" and "we" in the "I or me."

Metaphorically, our lion (power, fierceness, and ferociousness) now tamed, has not eaten the lamb, but has lain down with the lamb (compassion and gentleness). The lion and lamb are One. This was Jesus' original teaching, not the manipulated words in the Bible.

With the focus of our lion power now on compassionately creating and not furiously destroying, we are able to journey into the unknown with gentle power and face our fears with compassion. Peace be upon us and outside us.

Lion, Maiden, Tarot

For eons humans have gazed at the night sky with awe and wonderment. For the earliest religious leaders and philosophers, the stars, and the moon, as well as nature, were teachers and seen as a source of knowledge and wisdom. To these wise ones the night sky was a starry script that could reveal the mysteries of life and death. With creative imagination, these wonderworkers assigned symbolic names for the various grouping of stars with the realization that "as above so below, as below so above." This was the knowledge of the oneness of heaven and earth—the one a reflection of the other.

In the night's angelic script there were thirteen groupings of stars known today as constellations. Two of these were named Leo and Virgo—the lion in the night sky was followed by the maiden. These two constellations and their symbolic images are the gist of the eleventh tarot card—The Tamed Lion: Power. Modern tarot decks have a propensity to use the exoteric name for this card and call it Strength. Additionally, in some modern decks, it is tarot card eight not eleven. But the esoteric number placement was eleven and the card's name was Power.

Love

The eleventh tarot card symbolizes power. And what is the greatest power—love. Love conquers all, even the king of the beasts. The eleventh tarot card symbolizes the transmutation of the energy of the beast within—through love. This is the card of the mastery of one's self and one's own actions. It portrays a maiden with her hands on the open jaws of the lion symbolizing that she has tamed the beast. It is only through the maiden's "loving acceptance of its bestial nature that the animal is not only tamed but is transformed as well.... when human consciousness recognizes and accepts its untamed, primitive nature, it not only frees itself from the instinct's autonomous power but liberates and transforms the instinctual side as well."[142]

With gentle hand and eye, she charms the beast
And teaches him the time to speak. Released
From fear of one another, freedom grows
For each. A bond that blossoms like the rose.
It's love, not force or fear, that tames the beast![143]

The lion represents instinct while the maiden symbolizes reason. The beastly aggressions may be tamed by the "gentle application of conviction-in-reason, firmness requiring no more effort than the fact of the thought itself. Love will therefore conquer hate, good will over-come evil. The positive constitutes an invincible barrier, like a wall, as Gandhi said, that can neither be breached nor tumbled."[144]

* * *

As the eleventh tarot card, the lion and the maiden are connected with the eleventh letter of the Greek alphabet—Lambda, which sym-bolizes balance. Once again, we see the importance of balance and harmony. In this case it means a balanced use of power. This is the ability to know when to let our lion roar, when to let it be silent and when to "unleash" its power.

When we tame the beast within, our behaviors become empathic and altruistic—pro-social behavior.[145] We become responsible for our actions and our behaviors. The key is once again the relationship of self and other—being responsible and caring means that we will not hurt anyone else through our actions, such as not wearing a mask.

However, we do not metaphorically become a saint. We still have the basic primal instinctive survival, safety, and sexual wants and needs. Through the process of taming our beast, we are able to sustain our beneficial strength and power (i.e. protection of loved ones) while letting go of some of our destructive behaviors, but possibly, not all. The ones not let go we symbolically "press them down" or "bind them."

Pressing Down or Binding

Divine Humanity believes in an interpenetration of all aspects of reality. This means the darkness that we have within us has both constructive and destructive sides. They are not separate but interpen-etrated. In other words, even if we awaken our beast within, we have still not separated our constructive side from our destructive side. The destructive side is still there and could at some future time raise its ugly head. This is one of the times where "pressing down or binding" comes in handy.

Pressing down or binding means keeping inappropriate actions and behaviors under control where they are never or seldom acted upon. It means that the urge is still there, but it is not acted upon. This is not an act of suppression. It does mean that one is not acting on or repeating destructive behaviors.

There are dysfunctional and possible destructive emotions, behaviors, and thought processes that with fortitude we can let them go or transform them. It is not a dualistic "either-or" reality. There will be ones that cannot be transformed. Instead, they need to be pressed-down or bound. This means keeping inappropriate first chakra actions and behaviors under control where they are still there but are never acted upon. This is vividly symbolized by the Archangel Mikaël pressing down by standing on the dragon and its destructive (unawaken) energy of the first chakra.

Guardians

Just as the lion is the animal guardian or co-essence of Herakles, we may also have a co-essence. This energetic essence helps increase our power within. Co-essences may take many forms, even thunder and/or lightning. But many times, the form is an animal. Whatever form, a co-essence is a powerful companion for us in our journey to awaken. These guardians may help us become closer to nature and its seemingly wild and untamed forces. We are never truly alone in our journey of life. Our guardians are our constant companions as well as our helpers. A hummingbird guardian may help us move faster on our feet, whereas a serpent guardian may help us internally release/shed our past that is inhibiting our happiness and growth in the present. A jaguar guardian may help us achieve a fearless state of mind that will help us through this pandemic.

Guardians may come to us in our dreams. One benchmark is the occurrence of the same animal or creature in a dream. This must happen three times—the appearance of the same creature. The appearances must not be spread over months, but must occur within a short period of time. Once we have bonded with a guardian, we need to put our attention on it: • Discover its name; ask what it would like to be called • Research knowledge and facts about this guardian's species • Collect pictures and objects of your guardian • Honor your guardian on a daily basis; pray with it, go for a walk with it, spend time with it • Never kill or eat your guardian's species e.g. shark—do not kill or harm or let others do the same to a shark and do not eat shark meat.

Creative Imagination and Visualization

We complete this step with an important ability to increase the power of our heart, mind, and spirit—creative imagination, the power of visualization. Utilizing creative imagination will help us achieve a "strong mind." This is the power of creative imagination. It is considerably vast and can provide us a never-ending journey of exploration and the potential to experience whatever we can visualize.

To awaken from a dualistic consciousness to a consciousness of radical non-duality, a beginning step is the ability to maintain an image within our minds for a period of time without the disruptive influence of mind-chatter—a meditative mind, the power of meditation which overcomes distracted thought. This is the ability to concentrate with focus, intent, and will. This means being alone with ourselves—no outside stimuli such as smart phones. This is precisely a condition for the ability to love and an essential process in our awakening. The following is a beginning visualization:

Rose Visualization

Since time immemorial, the rose has been a symbol of love, life, beauty, and joy mystically expressing the qualities necessary for awakening and rebirth.

Preparation—find a quiet place where you will not be disturbed (by ringing phones, interruptions, etc.) in your home or out in nature. Have your journal nearby so that you can record your experience in it as soon as you complete the visualization. Be as comfortable as possible and totally relaxed. If you have incense or sage, you may burn this, but it is not necessary. Sit up in a comfortable position and start doing slow deep breathing from your belly. Let your eyes gradually close. Continue deep breathing, slowly; visualize the air coming in through the top of your head and going out through your navel region. ....Feel yourself relaxing. (This is also a breathing technique for relaxation, present moment awareness, and stress reduction.)

Visualization—identify with all of your senses every sound that you can hear. Hear your breathing; hear your heart beating. Identify all the different sounds.... Next, identify all the different feelings. What do you feel? Are your clothes soft? Identify what you feel.... Now, what do you smell? Identify the scents around you.... Lastly, what do you taste? Identify all the tastes....

Now visualize a rose bud in your heart. What color is it? Stay with this image for as long as possible. When complete, tell yourself to remember this experience; then slowly open your eyes and record your experience in your journal.

Progression—at your own pace, slowly and progressively transform the rosebud into a fully opened rose. As the rose bud opens a small spark of the divine will be in the center of the rose. Further opening transforms the spark into a flame of light.

Progressively utilize all of your senses with this visualization, the color of the rose, the smell, the feeling within your heart, the smell of the spark, its color, and so forth until the rose is fully open then consistently maintain this visualization of the open rose of fire and light for as long as needed.

3. ACCEPT A GREEN PHILOSOPHY

Experience and Embrace the Magic of Mother Nature

Moyers: ... What happens when human beings destroy
their environment?
Destroy their world? Destroy nature and the revelations of nature?
Campbell: They destroy their own nature, too. They kill the song.
Moyers: And isn't mythology the story of the song?
Campbell: Mythology is the song. It is the song of the
imagination, inspired by the energies of the body.[146]

There is one key element and one especially important concept that permeate the belief and philosophy of indigenous cultures and Divine Humanity. This is the belief in the importance of nature by forming a partnership and a oneness with nature—a nature that is divine, alive, conscious, and responsive. This makes sense since the earth is a sentient being—alive and conscious. Nature is the Holy Grail of healing and the secret to the maintenance of wholeness and wellness for all individuals, communities, and nations.

Even though the Grail is enigmatic in its identity, it is essential to understand that the Holy Grail is not an item to possess. It is not an external "thing." It is our awakening and awakened hearts and minds and in a grand sense it symbolizes what has been lost—humanity's, and our own, lost values. The primarily one is the loss of the feminine (nature) and the equality of men and women. This is the lost Feminine Principle (Mother Nature terrestrial and celestial) of the cosmos—the seen world. This world of ours only recognizes as authentic the light, not the dark; the material, not the spiritual; the male principle, not the feminine. This is then the quest—the quest to recover the feminine and nature—to heal the "wound" of the separation, suppression, abuse, and control of the feminine.

The subtle energies, which we may consider "magical," are "in reality perfectly natural. Nature herself is the greatest scientist, and in her daily displays of miraculous events show us the result of her experiments."[147] More than one of the ingenious shamans and healers that have we studied with for over thirty years, all said the same thing: "For every human ill, there is a cure in nature."

Nature is extremely important to the philosophy of Divine Humanity and without a doubt, nature is Kulana Huli Honua.[148]

Religion and spiritual teachings can never be separated from nature—the primary teacher is always nature. Religion and spiritual studies are supposed to explore and seek knowledge about the mysteries of life, death, and creation. This seeking of truth, about these mysteries and the pursuit of a fulfilled life and happiness, cannot be found in a book, no matter if some human says it is the "word of God;" nor can it be found within human made structures—it can only be found in nature and our relationship to the earth and to the heavens. The true foundation of any church or religious structure is the green earth and sapphire studded sea with the roof being the blue sky above. Most appropriate this concept is during the pandemic.

Divine Humanity believes that Oneness cannot be known through theory only through experience where we gain direct "intuition of the essential oneness of the macrocosm and microcosm… direct intuition of the fact that the macrocosm—the universe or Mother Nature—and oneself are essential one."[149] In other words, "nature and the universe are not thought of as being objectified existences apart from oneself. Nature and the universe are not inert things, for they are seen as existences which have a single life. In Esoteric Buddhism, the universe which includes all things such as human beings, plants, animals, and the natural environment are all referred to as being Mah vairocana -Tath gata the Cosmic Buddha embracing life."[150]

As we know within our hearts, Mother Nature is wondrous, magical, and a miracle of creation. The universe as Mother Nature is a great concept to embrace. It expands our concern and consciousness for the well-being of all things out to the stars. This takes the religious philosophical concept of the kingdom of God from just being earthbound out to the stars—the totality of the universe!

Having our heart and nature as one essence is essential for our well-being of body, mind, and spirit. Our heart will assist us in connecting with nature, and nature will help us be connected to our heart—a blending of love.

Partnership

Humanity in partnership with nature is essential for the survival and the renewal of humanity. In addition, a oneness with nature is primary in awakening and ascension. Nature in partnership is one of the hallmarks of Divine Humanity. It acknowledges the equality and divinity of nature and the realization that humanity is not above nature, as a steward, or below nature, at the mercy of it, but is one with nature and in partnership with the earth in co-creating a paradisiacal state of life, for all life.

The Church, Science, Capitalism, and our consumer society have supported and encouraged the superiority of humanity over nature. In their self-serving views, they have promoted a separation paradigm as proper, biblical, justifiable, and necessary for the progress of the human race.

In their arrogance, they have basically stirred up a hornet's nest. In their egotistical self-importance, the few greedily increase their wealth at the expense of the poor and the earth. They tell people climate change is a hoax as the masses, being the masses, follow as sheep while being led to the crumbling edge of an unstable mountainous cliff. Please understand that the Earth, Mother Nature, listens to humans' words and thoughts and responds accordingly. Considering the results of climate change, the recent destructive fires and the clouds of smoke choking the West Coast and the destructive hurricane seasons—She's finally fed up. Without drastic change humanity is doomed—is the coronavirus Mother Nature's Revenge?

Return to a Green Philosophy

We Sami people have lived here longer than we remembered to carry.
We haven't come here from somewhere. We've always been here.
Guest, this country is not ours, and this country is not yours.
And these waters are not ours, and these waters are not yours either. This country belongs to no one.
Guest listen to us now. Our mother's country, which is so dear to us, takes care of us, as it has taken care of our ancestors, which will allow us to live here as saamelaisina people.
Guest hear this again. New generations need to continue our lifestyle after our days.
You Guest, who have invaded our ancestors' ancient lands: you have no respect for our ancestor's lifestyle, our livelihood, our language, nor our culture. You don't appreciate what's on earth. You only want what is a mother in the depths of our country and what you have no right to.
Guest, do you know that the country has always been the source of the wealth of our lives.
We respect the country, our mother. Because it gives us life.
You Guest, do not respect our wealth, vulnerable nature, and clean waters.

They mean nothing to you. And you want to destroy our lifestyle
by harming the country, our mother.
We can't live without the country, our mother, nor without the
father, our sun.
A visitor. Do you want to kill our mother, earth?
Do you want to erase our lives? Or do you want to kill us
Sami people?
A visitor. Before you go, listen to these ancestors joikuja[151] again.
They are about our lives and our treasures. They tell you why our
lives are so rich.
They tell us that we and our children still have land, our mother.[152]

Listen to the Sami. Like them, we believe and live a Green Philosophy. This is an egalitarian philosophy of humanity's partnership with the seen and unseen things of the Earth and nature. Humans are part of nature, not at the center of nature. Furthermore, society has lost many of the values treasured by past indigenous cultures, such as a partnership with nature, truth telling, and elder/ancestor respect and honor. We need to discover meaning in life, not accumulate money and material things. The equality of men and women as well as the equality of all things—as all have the starlight/divine spark within them—needs to be reinstated. These and other lost values need to be reinstated throughout this Earth. Nature needs to be respected, loved, and cared for by humanity. We need to be partners in relationship with nature, not its stewards. We need your help. We would ask that you join us and Sami in embracing a Green Philosophy of life and spread this knowledge to others. And most importantly, support climate-change initiatives and do your part in stopping and reversing climate-change.

Heart and Nature as One

Someone who has not found the vine cannot pick the fruit,
and someone
who has not "found" the earth cannot plant the vine!
—Rev. Dr. JC Husfelt (1997)

Earth is a paradise of wonders all wrapped up in a multitude of colors. It is alive, consciousness responding to all the things that call it home. I believe in a partnership with the earth and feel at one with it. How about you? Have you ever taken the time to go out into nature, away from human encroachment, and just set on the earth and feel the beauty and love surrounding you? Have you ever taken the time to see "elf and dwarf" peer forth from field and stone? Have you considered that you have no other reason than to just be part of and in partnership with nature; no smart phones or tablets, no hiking from point to point, but just you, and the Great Mother—listening, seeing, feeling, smelling, and even tasting the essence of the kingdom of nature?

When was the last time you viewed the miracle of sunrise; the wonder of sunset; the magical rise of the moon in its fullness, reminding you of the interpenetration of light within dark? Have you ever been in awe of the darkness of a new moon, knowing that all growth is born out of darkness? When are you going to awaken to the paradise spread before you?

When I talk about Mother Nature, I'm referring not only to the earth but also to the whole of the seen and unseen universe as stated in Divine Humanity's Philosophical Approach to Cosmology and Ontology.[153] This philosophy is based on my soul knowledge using the Fibonacci sequence (1202 CE) which mirrors the Pythagoreans (Pythagoras c. 570 - c. 495 BCE). Divine Humanity acknowledges that the Creator, the Unknown and the Uncreated, cannot be identified or imagined by the human mind and cannot be put into human terms, just in absolute terms, as it is the greatest mystery of all mysteries. The Absolute—the One—which Divine Humanity refers to as God, is beyond form and conception, the unmanifest. It is outside of time and space; in a sense it is timelessness.

For reasons beyond what any human mind may comprehend, the Absolute reflected itself—the Reflective Absolute. Philosophically, these are like two multifaceted jewels that refract and reflect in limitless combinations. The Pythagoreans relate the Absolute to the Monad and the Reflective Absolute to the Indefinite/Undetermined/Creative Dyad.

"Pythagoras said that the great Monad acts as a creative Dyad. Immediately God manifests himself, he is double; indivisible essence and divisible substance; active, animating, masculine principle, and passive, feminine principle, or animated plastic matter. Accordingly, the Dyad represented the union of the Eternal-Masculine and the Eternal-Feminine in God, the two essential and corresponding divine faculties. Orpheus had poetically expressed this idea in the line: Jupiter is the divine Bridegroom and Spouse.

"All polytheisms have intuitively been conscious of this idea, representing the Divinity under the masculine, sometimes under the feminine form. This living, eternal Nature, this mighty Spouse of God, is not only the terrestrial but also the celestial nature, invisible to our eyes of flesh, the Soul of the world, the primordial Light, in turn Maia, Isis or Cybele, who, first vibrating beneath the divine impulse, contains the essences of all souls, the spiritual types of all beings. Then it is Demeter, the living earth, and all earths with the bodies they enfold in which these souls have come to be incarnated. Afterwards it is Woman, the companion of Man. In humanity Woman represents Nature, and the perfect image of God is not Man alone, but Man and Woman."[154]

Flowers

The beauty of earth is permeated throughout with rainbow colors of love—flowers. Flowers are love. Who doesn't love flowers? The beauty and the scents permeate our soul and spirit. In a moment of darkness, flowers lift us in the spirit and light of joy and happiness. More so than ever, we each need this beauty and love within our homes, possibly brightening our depressed feelings. Now and after the pandemic, please bring nature/flowers into your home at least once a week. It will help to a small degree in balancing your heart and mind.

Flowers express one of our three pillars of light, a flower heart. It opens our heart so that it can germinate into a flower—the mystic flower of light. With a flower heart, we express love from our heart and let others, as well as ourselves, view the beauty and the divine perfection that is the true essence of our hearts. Smell is a powerful sense. With a Flower Heart, our fragrance is pure, sweet, and soothing to ourselves and others. The Flower Heart is the Rose, the Blue Lily or Lotus Heart.

The Whisper of Nature

"Heaven is under our feet as well as over our heads," said Henry David Thoreau; and "Nature is full of genius, full of the divinity, so that not a snowflake escapes its fashioning hand."

Ironically, this pandemic may be the perfect time to visit and experience the purity of nature (the more isolated the better) as it is the best place to practice a detached non-chattering mind, to relax, and rejuvenate yourself. Common sense and reason would dictate this to be true. Mythologically, paradise has been viewed as nature—a garden, not as a building. Nature provides an abundance of negative-ions, which are beneficial to our health, level of stress, and well-being.

The beginning stage is to acclimate ourselves to our surroundings using all our senses to identify the area. First, it is best to do an "eagle-view" of the area, such as identifying all the sounds that we hear. Do this with each sense. Then shift to a "hawk-view" of nature. Identify your surroundings in detail. When you feel connected and relaxed begin the practice of a strong mind by focusing softly with your eyes on your surrounding but not attaching to or identify anything with any of your senses. Be totally aware with all your senses but do not attach by assigning identification or judgments to them. Take as long as you feel comfortable. After a period of time, practice meditative thought. Complete by blessing and thanking the things of nature and their beauty. For this exercise to be successful, it needs to be repeated more than once—over-and-over again.

Nature Smiles

Eddie Pu, a Hawaiian friend of ours, taught me how to swim with the sharks. Eddie expressed the Aloha spirit and was called "Smiling Eddie" due to his eternal smile. His smiling, he explained, reflected nature. "When the wind blows, the leaves are waving—they're smiling. When you throw a rock into a pool and the ripples go out—the water is smiling. That's the energy. That's what I call my energy."[155]

Listening to Eddie, let your smile reflect the energy of nature. The next time the wind blows, watch the leaves smile, and smile back. Feel, embrace, and be this loving energy of nature.

Nature Spirits

Nature spirits are real. These land spirits—the elementals who are everywhere and are an embodiment of nature itself—must be respected. According to the Norse-Germanic tradition, *Landvættir* are the land spirits linked with the land itself. Being in friendship/ partnership and honoring the *landvættir* could bring prosperity to a family in farming, hunting, and fishing. Additionally, they provided protection to the children and animals.

To honor them, we need to gift them. This gifting could take the form of alcohol left for them or poured on the earth, or incense/sacred herbs burned as a gift of sweet essence. Even leaving a few flowers (ask their permission to be picked) on the ground would be a right action. Finally, a small sacrifice as a gift—pull some hair and leave it on the earth. End with thankfulness and a blessing for the well-being of all the unseen ones.[156]

Ancestral guardians – *'Aumākua*

A Hawaiian fisherman would acknowledge his 'aumākua, the shark, before casting his net.

Ancestral guardians are of the earth, and for some cultures, are an indispensable part of life. These guardians are the spirits of the family lineage that protect and guide the people as well as form a sacred bond between the land and the people. Ancestral guardians provide a legacy of sacredness that guides the people to a oneness of being with the earth, not separateness from the earth. Ancestral guardians connect people to the land. When this spiritual principle is not an integral part of a culture, the earth and its inhabitants are deemed expendable. This is exactly what has happened, and is happening today, resulting in an ecological catastrophe; the ramifications of which are still unknown. When people feel separate and cut off from their ancestral lineage and heritage, the spirituality of the earth, as well as the values that it provides, become hollow, vague and in most cases, non-existent.

All is not lost if, and only if, we return to the sacredness of the land and look to the spirituality and values that are such an integral part of earth cultures—such as the Hawaiians where the elders (kupuna) were honored and revered. It was the kupuna who brought forth the voice of the ancestors. They were the well-source of wisdom and knowledge for the people of Hawaii. They taught the people and "talked story" about the ancestral guardians and taught that the ancestors could manifest in physical form. The closest human-with-god relationship came in the *'aumākua*. The bond between humans and *'aumākua* was very real and might take the animal form of owl, shark, and turtle, to name a few.

'Aumākua may also be viewed as our divine self. To the ancient Hawaiians, all healing is the result of a natural communion with our divine-self. Accordingly, joyful cooperation with "god-in-everything" is the best medicine for all ills, the best solution to all problems, the best way to achieve personal fulfillment. To do this, however, takes a commitment to remind yourself constantly of the presence of God in all people, places, things and situations.[157]

Animals – Consciousness with a Divine Spark

Animals are conscious beings with a divine spark/fire within them. Do not harm them. Research has resulted in the "Cambridge Declaration on Consciousness signed by 16 well-known scientists, some of whom do or have done invasive research, concluded:

> Convergent evidence indicates that non-human animals have the neuroanatomical, neurochemical, and neurophysiological substrates of conscious states along with the capacity to exhibit intentional behaviors. Consequently, the weight of evidence indicates that humans are not unique in possessing the neurological substrates that generate consciousness. Non-human animals, including all mammals and birds, and many other creatures, including octopuses, also possess these neurological substrates.[158]

Embracing the Power of Nature

To embrace the power of nature, consider planting a tree, such as an apple tree or fig tree that represents both vitality and enlightenment, to honor one of your ancestors or family members, or plant a tree as a guardian tree of your land as a honoring to the land spirits.

Constructing a stone circle on your land would be an honoring and a sacred place for meditation. The stone circle does not need to have the stones touching each other. In fact, a more sacred way is a few large stones that form a circle or oval. This is witnessed by ancient stone circles such as the Ring of Brodgar on the Orkney Islands and Avebury in England. The Ring is 5,000 years old. This is older than Stonehenge and the great pyramids of Egypt. Far traveling to both of these sacred sites, I can attest to their power and purity.

Ring of Brodgar

Considering the pandemic, instead of running to a store, adventure out to an isolated place in nature where you could find large stones such as by a stream. Ask permission to take them, leave a gift, and take them home to build a sacred circle.

Additionally, sacred outdoor space may be as simple as a large stone or a certain tree that is special to you. At the base of the tree or stone, you can lay a flat stone that you could find in nature or safely purchase at a garden supply center. On this flat stone, you could place an incense bowl. This would signify the tree or stone as sacred space. Do not worry about doing wrong. As long as you are doing it from your heart and not your unhealthy ego, there is no wrong.

Ho'okupu

The Hawaiian concept *ho'okupu* means "to cause growth" as well as "ceremonial gift-giving." Typically, *ho'okupu* is in the form of a plant. Metaphorically, you want to cause growth through the *ho'okupu*. The gift can be a flower (something organic) or as simple as a prayer with the intent of causing growth while giving something unconditionally back to the land, to sacred space, and/or to the unseen and seen sacred ones.

Listen with Heart and Mind...

to our connection to nature. When we listen, we learn from nature; it points us to our inner nature, a knowing of our sacred heart and the divine within us. Birds sing to us if we only listen with a silence of mind. Birds call and sing not only to quicken plants, but also sing to us to awaken and quicken our divine seed within our hearts. When we listen to what the birds have to say, to what nature has to say, and when we perceive the beauty of nature, then we are on the edge of awakening our divine consciousness.

In the Old Norse tradition, bird-speech was not so foreign. Special individuals capable of understanding the language of birds are spread throughout the medieval Icelandic literary corpus. Capable of flight and song, birds universally hold a special place in human experience. Their effective communication to people in Old Norse lore offers another example of their unique role in humanity's socio-cosmic reality. One of the myths concerns the dragon Fáfnir and Sigurðr. After slaying the dragon *Fáfnir* and tasting its blood, Sigurðr comprehends the speech of birds.[159]

Another method to experience a connection with nature is for our skin to touch the earth. Remove your shoes and walk with bare feet on the sacred earth. Sit and lie upon the earth to feel its energetic force or, even better, bare yourself to the earth. This allows us to see more clearly and feel kinship with all things near us. Everything has an intrinsic personality. Before we can talk to birds, trees, or stones, we must first listen to them. The world is our library, encoded within the stones, leaves, grass, brooks, seas, fjords, and animals—all things of nature's paradise. The closer we are to nature, the nearer we are to the beauty and truth of our hearts. If there is a lack of respect for nature, then there will be a lack of respect for other human beings and needless destruction of nature.

Working Humbly with the Elements

"Aloha e ka lā, e ka lā!
E ola mai e ka lā, i ka Honua nei."
Greetings to the sun, life, the earth."[160]

There are six elements: earth, water, fire, wind/air, space, and consciousness, which are eternally and unchangeably blended. Since the six elements are mutually blended, the physical five elements wholly permeate the sixth element, consciousness. This in turn means consciousness wholly pervades each of the five physical elements.

Physical things and mental things blend together—mental things mean both "heart" and "mind."

In other words, the elements are alive and conscious, meaning we are able to "speak" and work with them. Being humble and thankful is important. Asking permission before entering the wilderness, picking an herb or flower, or intruding upon nature in any way is an essential practice. When you ask permission of nature and give thanks for its bounty, you are acknowledging spirit in all things and practicing a reverence for life.[161] When we have a reverence for life, life/nature responds to us.

Fire

Fire as a transformative energy is simultaneously destructive and creative. Its power begins, sustains, and ends life. It initiates life by providing the vivifying spark of life and sustains life by contributing life-giving warmth. The Norse believed that fire took people and materials to the Otherworld. As truth, Sher and I know this as we carry the medicine power of a burning, feeding the Otherworld. Furthermore, I carry the medicine power of transformational fire ceremonies. We know the power of fire.

Symbolically, Fire represents the Absolute/Heaven while Water corresponds to the Relative/Earth. Metaphorically, the blending of the opposites of Fire and Water results in harmony and a Oneness of Self. This blending of fire and water is the awakening of the divine spark, a consciousness of radical nonduality, with an inner feeling permeating the body of icy fire. To experience the magic of fire yourself, build a small fire and be in silence with a strong mind while maintaining the intent to experience its magic. Stare into the flames. This might lead from "wandering reverie to mystical revelation; the energy of the Universe is being released and mystically transformed, like the symbolism of the phoenix rising from the ashes. In the incandescent colours and fiery sparks one might see the vital interaction of natural forces, combining to create an alchemical transmutation from physical to ethereal. It may even be possible to sense the Divine Spark within."[162] Record your experience when you are finished.

Green Man, Green One or Gardener

A commonly accepted word for humanity's connection to nature is the "Green Man." The Green Man or Gardener is a powerful mythic image known to every civilization. He is depicted with vegetation symbolizing the Life Force or Word of God spewing from his mouth.

The Gardener symbolizes fertility, eternity, death and rebirth. The archetypical Green Man or Gardener may be visualized as a human face peering through vegetation or possibly as a mystical mixture of human form and vegetation merging into each other. This imagery of the Green Man symbolizes a portal to the Otherworld, a connection between humanity and nature. The Green Man is that spirit, energy, and presence inherent in every cell of the vegetative realm and transmitted to the animal/human realms through the foods we eat, the flowers we smell, the trees we hug.

The Green Man calls us to learn from the earth. When the earth is our teacher, we will be drawn more fully to honor, nourish and protect her. In other words, "Nature is our teacher not merely in physical form but is also completely at one with our inner being. The Green Man symbolizes this unity of inner nature and Mother Nature. As Emerson says, 'Nature is the symbol of the spirit.' By learning to be enlightened readers of nature's sacred manuscript, we can attune our hearts to knowledge on how to take care of the Earth. As we each awaken to our true nature within, we can spread and share the consciousness of the Green Man, become the Gardener, and bring compassion and caring to the Earth."[163]

We are the Gardener

Mythologically, paradise has long been viewed as nature—a garden paradise. Personal and community gardens are important, especially considering the lack of quality and hormone ingrained commercial food. Locally grown food increases our health and wellbeing.

Our gardens are not only external. Each of us has a potential garden within us. We are the Gardener within. To discover your garden, please do the following meditation/visualization:

❖ THE PREPARATION: Find a quiet place where you will not be disturbed in your home or out in nature. Be as comfortable as possible and totally relaxed. You may burn incense or a plant such as sage, but it is not necessary. You may also put on a drumming cassette tape, or some other repetitive sound tape, such as bells or gongs. Again, this is not necessary; these are just aids to help you quiet the internal dialogue, or "chatter," within your mind, and to help you begin journeying.

   You may sit on the floor, on the ground, in a chair, or even lie down. Choose a posture that will be comfortable, but not tiring or conducive to falling asleep.

❖ THE BEGINNING: Once you are ready to begin start by noticing your surroundings. Use all of your senses to do this: see something very clearly (the floor), hear something (your heartbeat), smell something (the air), feel something (your arm), and taste something (use your tongue to taste your upper lip).

   Now start paying attention to your breathing. As you breathe in, visualize the air coming in through the crown of your head, and as you exhale, visualize the air leaving by your navel region. Maintain this shifting of your awareness...breathe in air through the crown, breathe out air through the navel. In a few seconds, let your eyes close, and feel how relaxed you feel.

❖ THE MEDITATION: Go within and visualize creating a Garden. Put whatever is special to you in your Garden. It could be an oriental garden, or a traditional English garden, a garden you had as a child, or a present garden. You may have a waterfall or other water source, such as a pond, within your garden that may be crisscrossed with paths of stone or grass. Even a sacred stone circle. Whatever is special to you... Use all of your senses to develop your Garden... What do you see, what do you hear, what do you smell, what do you feel, what do you taste?

You are the Gardener. Be sure to keep your Garden healthy, growing with flowers, trees, and even vegetables. Your Garden is the inner reflection of your outward self. Use love and care in tending your Garden. Please go into your garden and spend time there. It would be best to do this on a daily basis.

❖ THE CONCLUSION: As with all experiential exercises and meditations, it is best to lock the experience away within your subconscious, either by writing it down, or discussing it with another person, or both. You may also want to draw or sketch your garden.

The Music of Trees

dod yn ol at fy nghoed
Welsh phrase meaning "to return to a balanced state of mind" –
translates literally as "to return to my trees."

The standing sentinels of our world whose roots bury deep within the body of the Great Mother and whose bare or green-covered branches reach towards the sky provide life and beauty for all. The grandeur Sher and I have experienced on forested mountain tops and in verdant valleys has brought us joy and peace of mind and memories that are priceless.

Trees, like all other things, are conscious and aware. In fact, they communicate with each other and will listen to our words and thoughts. "Two decades ago, while researching her doctoral thesis, ecologist Suzanne Simard discovered that trees communicate their needs and send each other nutrients via a network of latticed fungi buried in the soil – in other words, she found they 'talk' to each other. Since then, Simard, now at the University of British Columbia, has pioneered further research into how trees converse, including how these fungal filigrees help trees send warning signals about environmental change, search for kin, and transfer their nutrients to neighboring plants before they die."[164]

It seems that few humans understand the impact of the gifts that trees provide to the Earth and humanity, and intrinsically, every tree has its own unique song. A vibrational and harmonic essence of its "soul"—an eternal divine starlight of perfection. To discover a tree's song, first we must believe that trees have consciousness. Second, we dialogue with the tree, bless it, and become familiar with each other. Dialogue is not only verbal but with images in our mind that match our words. This needs to happen for a period, possibly weeks or months before the tree is open to share its song.

To discover the song, bless and honor the tree, kiss the tree, and hug it. Ask permission if it is willing to share its song with you. If so, then sit at its base with your back and head on its trunk, quiet your mind and listen.... Listen and then begin humming its song... when complete, thank and bless the tree stating that you will honor it by singing/humming its song on a regular basis. Finally, give-gift something back to the tree. And do not forget the tree, bless it, its song, and its essence and presence every so often.

Nature Welcomes Us

Training in nature, far away from the irritations and distractions of modern life, will help us uncover the body-mind that is so important in awakening. is not the body and mind of dualistic thinking, but body/mind—the actual experience and being of the oneness of life. With the sky overhead and the

earth beneath our feet, we may experience what the Norse of old felt—nature as school. But remember that nature and the earth are unforgiving of one's unhealthy ego and stupidity. Common sense as well as preparation is indispensable in nature's wildness. Many people lack directional sense, and even if you do have a good sense of direction, a compass, a map, and the knowledge of how to use them are essential. If you choose to go alone into a wilderness area, it is best to let someone know where you are going and your expected time of return. Water, a knife, matches or lighter, and a day pack with a change of clothes, extra socks, and some fruit and trail mix are a good idea if you are planning on spending the day out in nature; in addition, be informed of the local weather conditions. One further point, the preceding is of utmost importance as the power to survive is to be found within ourselves. In other words, a smart phone may be included with your items, but do not totally be dependent on it. Look to yourself not technology.

Once you are in nature, there are many methods that will help you develop and strengthen your spirit and wisdom. I will suggest a few basic exercises that I have used with our students.

Listen, Look, Learn, and Know

❖ A meditative walk using all your senses except your eyes, which can switch from half closed to fully closed to fully open. Our eyes happen to be one of the prime gateways for spiritual afflictions or attachments to occur in our mind. The majority of people's eyes normally see, and what they see they attach to, thus arresting the mind and allowing desires, judgments, fears, and many other mind afflictions to arise.

Our goal is to listen and see with our hearts as well as with our metaphoric third eyes, or intuitive eyes, which are above our physical eyes and centered in our foreheads, and connect us with the pituitary and pineal glands in the brain.

❖ A quest in nature would be another tool to help you in discovering self-knowledge. This involves nothing more than just sitting or, a little harder, standing in one spot for two or more hours. This means just being with ourselves with the sky and the earth as witnesses without moving or doing anything. Sitting against the base of a tree would be very enlightening, as the tree has its roots in the earth and its branches reaching toward the sky, symbolizing the unity of and connection between sky and earth.

Listen to the tree; then commune with it. Sit in silence for a period of time. After your mind is calm and without mind chatter, you may begin visualizing and feeling your energy within your spine merging with the tree's energy. Practice moving this merged energy up, and then descending down your spine and within the tree's trunk.

After practicing the above for a few weeks, a more advanced exercise involves standing with your back and full body against an elder (older) tree. First, ask permission of the tree for you to work with its body and soul. If permission is granted, first hug the tree for a few minutes then stand with your back and full body against the tree. Begin slow breathing while maintain the awareness of all sensory input. Slowly close your eyes. After a few seconds begin visualizing a light in the center of your brain (pineal gland); keep being aware of all your senses. Slowly descend this light down your spine until it merges with the base of your spine (sacrum and coccyx). There are nine segments of the sacrum (5) and coccyx (4). Nine is the sacred number of humans. The pineal gland is our potential pine cone of light. When it awakens, our number becomes ten—the sacred number of divine human beings.

Maintain this column of light flowing from your pineal gland to your sacrum and coccyx. This flow is both descending and ascending. Listen and feel the soul of the tree. Let it feel your soul. After a period of time let your body and soul merge with the trees body and soul. Feel, and be, the essence of the tree and yourself as one. However, always keep a ten percent awareness of your separate self. After a period of time, let your internal column of light descend through your feet and down through the roots of the tree and then ascend this sacred light up from the roots of the tree through you and continuing up to the very top of the tree. Be one with all things. Maintain this interconnectedness for a period of time. When ready feel your body and soul physically separating from the tree. Be aware of all of your senses. Slowly open your eyes and observe your surroundings. As a completion, thank and bless the tree, its body and soul. Kiss it and give a gift back to it. This gifting may be as simple as some of your hair placed on the trunk of the tree or sacred ale poured on the trunk and around its base. Keep this memory alive within your heart and mind.

❖ Finally, be respectful of all things (e.g., do not litter and give thanks when you leave for your safety and all that you have learned and experienced).

Mandala of Nature

The word mandala is a Sanskrit term that means "circle." It is usually a circular design containing concentric geometric forms, images of deities, etc. and symbolizing the universe, totality, or wholeness/oneness. Mandalas are used as a focus tool for meditation.

There are different types of mandalas, such as an "action" or "movement" mandala. Two examples of these mandalas include the breath of the wind and the gurgling of a stream. They have an important symbolic significance as they are manifestations of the activity of the universe.

Having this knowledge, plan on going to a flowing stream to mediate while focusing on the movement of the stream, its sounds and your feelings with the intent of becoming one with the stream (the universe).

Nature — Garden Paradise of Love: Oneness with Nature

❖ Acknowledge and believe that all things, including nature, have a consciousness and are alive and responsive.

❖ Spend consistent alone time just being with nature, not in a separate way but as a part of nature.

❖ See and acknowledge the beauty of nature and its children (creatures).

❖ Plant a flower garden.

❖ Plan and assist in a community garden.

❖ Listen to a tree and converse with it.

❖ Kiss trees, flowers, plants and so-forth.

❖ Talk to the winds and the winds will talk back.

❖ See the oneness and beauty of even the smallest creatures of earth.

❖ Walk softly over the earth and consciously harm no things.

❖ Have pets if possible.

❖ Let your yard grow naturally; do not use chemicals on it and do not

❖ make it a miniature golf course.

❖ Before cutting trees (only if necessary) or picking fruit off the vine, ask permission and give blessings.

❖ Have as many plants and flowers as possible in your living space.

❖ Garden with loving care.

❖ If possible, have a vegetable and/or herb garden.

❖ Eat organically and pressure society to make organically grown food affordable for all people.

- Eat locally grown or raised food as often as possible.

- Walk often and be with nature.

- Bless the overcast sky as well as the clear, blue sky; bless the sun and the moon; bless the wind and the rain.

- If possible, spend time with your family in nature.

- Bless nature and its importance to all daily.

- Increase the time that you normally spend outdoors.

- Walk barefoot on the earth.

- Forgo a hat or umbrella during rain and experience heaven's sweat and tears on your head—no rain, no rainbows.

- Listen, look, and learn from nature.

- Be one with the ocean and the sea; sit by a fjord and experience the power and wonder.

- These are just a few guidelines—what others can you add?

Our modern age of sterility is not healthy for us. This separation mentality is dysfunctional and unhealthy. Our bodies need bacteria. Their presence helps our systems stay healthy and balanced. So, go outside, be in close relationship with nature's paradise, and get dirty!

We are a part of everything that is beneath us, above us, and around us. Our past is our present, our present is our future, and our future is seven generations past and present.
—Haudenosaunee teaching

One additional point concerning, "all our relations." "Native American teachings describe the relations all around— animals, fish, trees, and rocks—as our brothers, sisters, uncles, and grandpas. Our relations to each other, our prayers whispered across generations to our relatives, are what bind our cultures together. The protection, teachings, and gifts of our relatives have for generations preserved our families. These relations are honored in ceremony, song, story, and life that keep relations close—to buffalo, sturgeon, salmon, turtles, bears, wolves, and panthers. These are our older relatives—the ones who came before and taught us how to live."[165]

4. EXPERIENCE THE MOMENT-TO-MOMENT MAGIC OF LOVE AND LIFE

Heart of Love

Deep inside my sacred body
There is a vessel that
Holds my memories
Of Forever...
Where Pain, Sorrow, Hurt, Loss,
Regret, Joy, Happiness, Peace and
Love share this ever growing
Heart - space...
With each soft beat and murmur
I receive - and - I release -
And - I bless the miracles
Of my life
~ Sher

Our next spiritual step is learning to live in the present—this breath, this heartbeat—in love and harmony. Some call this "being present" or a state of "mindfulness." It is important to keep in mind that power is now, in this moment, this day. Each day is a new day to love or hate, right action or wrong action, to be selfless and kind or to be selfish, narcissistic, and greedy.

A spiritual person of love and power lives in the present only visiting the past for healing unresolved circumstances and issues, and exploring the lessons learned from these past experiences. A spiritual person of love and power only journeys to the future to explore the potentialities of life.

Living in the past does not only mean the distant past, it also refers to the past day or even the past hour. Our minds have the unique ability to attach to the past and to the unknown future. If you think about it, it is philosophically and spiritually impossible to attach to the present, as each present moment turns into the past as each heartbeat marks the turning of the wheel of time. We can experience the present through our senses but as soon as we attach to the senses, the present moment is gone, and our attachment is to the immediate past.

To be present is to be aware of our sensory input without attachment, while letting the past moments flee from our present reality. Being aware of our breathing is important in helping us achieve the wonder and power of living now. Simply observing and blessing nature in all its beauty is another method for us to practice living in the now.

In this moment, bless and be happy, as it is our spiritual bouquet of roses. To bless is to honor and to acknowledge the divine light within all things. To bless is to spread the honey of our soul through a joyful message of caring praise and compassionate words. Blessing increases love—the essence of oneness.

When we live our lives in the present moment, we release our souls from being ever haunted by the past or ever fearful of the unknown future. This is the free will and power that we have within our grasp. Do not squander it.

More importantly, the present moment is a place of love and happiness. It is the magical moment that fills all of our senses with the smell of flowers and the sight of loved ones. It is beholding the awesomeness of a sunrise or a sunset and the beauty that surrounds us. So many miss the present due to their "chattering" mind—a mind that is constantly talking to itself. And the awareness of the present is nowhere to be found. To be present is to be aware.

Awareness

The awareness of the present moment comes through our senses. If our senses are dull, we experience little of the paradise and the flowery banquet that is set before us. We need to "listen, look and learn." This is always the key to power. If, on the contrary, our mind is chattering, we will truly not see or truly hear. If we are constantly talking and texting on a smartphone or posting on social media, our eyes become clouded and deluded while our minds become blocked to all sensory input. We miss life; we miss paradise; we suffer needlessly.

Do not continue down the same path of life. Yes, during this pandemic, we do miss our closeness and interactions with friends and other human beings. It is tough, it is a struggle. Keep in mind that "other" also means residents of nature and nature itself. Go outside and be one with nature. Being out in nature and being aware are essential to our sanity, growth, power, and love. We need to sit and smell the ground beneath us. We must stand and gaze at the tree in its totality and then see the shape of the leaves, the texture of the bark, and the bend of the limbs. We must crawl as a child on our Mother Earth while feeling, hearing, and seeing with our hearts the crawling ones invisible and meaningless to most ego-warped people, but meaningful, visible and consequential to us. We must listen for the passage of the serpent and the buzzing of the bees. The more we use our senses, the more we will stay in the present, the easier it will be to get through this pandemic; it is up to you. The choice is yours.

Web of Life

Photo by Sher

We are not "islands unto ourselves." We are all connected in a web of life that flows throughout creation. Consciousness, which is the sixth element, interpenetrates the other five elements of space, fire, air, water, and earth and travels along the treads of this cosmic divine web. In this way, we are literally the mind and eyes of God.

While we are each connected to the cosmic web, our degree of connectedness and our effect on each other does vary. This variance consists of different factors, among them, the relative physical distance between two persons or two things and their frequency of interaction. For example, the web of life's thread between my family and myself is stronger than the thread between myself and a stranger in China or myself and the star Sirius. Still, we are all connected and each one of our actions and reactions do affect all things. The stronger our focus and attention on something, the greater the connectedness between us and the other object. In other words, the energy flow between us and others is greatly enhanced.

Emotions generate great energy and increase our connectedness to others even if we do not want to be connected to them. When we feel a strong love for someone, or someone within our family, this increases our connectedness to them. That same amount of emotion in the form of hate for another person will also make the connection between the two people intensely strong. While this hate does affect the other individual to a small degree, the greatest debilitating effect to the body and mind is felt by the person doing the hating whether the emotion is justified or not. Here is where we enter the forgiveness zone. The process of forgiveness will resolve this hate and its debilitating effect. When we can speak or think about the other person with neutral emotions we know that forgiveness has truly been given and we are no longer damaging our body, mind, and spirit.

The web of life, as a philosophical premise, goes a long way in explaining many of the mysteries of life such as distant healing and how our words and thoughts do affect others as well as the earth. One of the best ways to increase our connectedness to others and the earth is through the heartfelt love of prayer and blessing.

With the dawn of each new day, our hearts, and souls trudge through a life of mundane patterns of being which have been encoded in our subconscious by a past that may seem more real than the present moment of our life. Cumulatively, the constant fear of an unknown future results in a non-spiritual, dis-empowered life of crinkled, mundane proportions. This is not the life we were meant to experience.

To awaken we must live in the present and only "visit" the past to heal, change dis-empowered patterns of behavior, and learn the lessons of wrong turns and missed opportunities. It is also important to learn from the mistaken and possibly wrong behaviors of ourselves and others.

An awakened person does not fear the future, but only "visions" the potentialities of life. To achieve this elevated essence of being takes courage, determination, and persistence. It is a struggle and not easy to change, to separate ourselves from the prevailing beliefs of society and the masses. It is much easier to go with societies' flow rather than follow our own hearts and common sense. But, and this is a big but, we need to be responsible for actions that may affect others (love thy neighbor as thyself). During this pandemic, the wearing of a mask is your responsibility. It is not only to protect you but to protect others from the virus as many people are asymptomatic. It is the same with social distancing. To abide by both takes personal responsibility, compassion, and kindness to others, and internal power. It is the right thing to do for the wellbeing of others and humanity.

* * *

To know God is to know ourselves and to know all other things—not only from our mind but also from our heart and our experience of life. It is as simple and as magical as lying on the earth while watching the clouds pass overhead. It is the breath of a baby. It is the overcast morn. It is the light that you may see in each other's eyes. And it is the volcano that destroys but in the same breath creates new land—baby earth.

Moment-to-moment, we need to keep in mind that the divine spark of God is within us and within all other things of creation. We need to be mindful of our connectedness and how our words, our actions, and our beliefs affect not only us but all other things as well.

Prayer

Let that which is unknown become known.[166]

It is important for prayer and blessing to be a natural part of our daily lives. They are our connection with the Otherworld as well as with nature. Prayer comes from our heart; in the moment, with the intention that the prayer has already been fulfilled. To the rest of creation there is neither a past nor a future, just the now—this present moment. Pray not in the past or the future, but in the present. Pray to the Divine Consciousness. Go directly to the source. Each morning we may pray by simply saying: "God, the One, the All, the Great Mystery: Thou Art, from whom the breath of life comes; who interpenetrates all realms of sound, light and vibration...."

Prayer is personal and not for the public display of one's unhealthy ego. It is the song, the language—communication with the Absolute and Relative of existence. To the Divine, every word and every thought is a prayer that vibrates through the golden streams of time and creation. Most importantly, our words, and even our thoughts, affect the earth and all its creatures.

We must be aware of our words and thoughts because each one does matter and may bring us, and others, joy or suffering. Every moment is sacred, and a life spent chattering in gossip, half-truths, and lies is a life squandered in dysfunctional darkness.

Lanakila Brandt, a Hawaiian Priest of *Lono*[167] taught that prayer generated *mana*, "*Mana* is life force, the power that enables us to live. ... The gift of *mana* is all of ours, and we can command this *mana*. You generate *mana* through prayer, through deep breathing and through meditation."[168]

* * *

Prayer is the inner silence that will reveal the inner truth of our hearts. This stillness guides us along the crystal-studded pathway of our soul's destiny. Spend time alone out in nature and listen with the ears of the heart to the chorus of angelic knowledge and you will know the oneness of heaven and earth.

A conscious prayer is like a seed that needs to be planted in good soil, watered, and nurtured. When the fruit of the seed is born, blessings, and gratitude are given.

On the other hand, many people pray as if they were lost in a desert sowing their seeds on the top of a barren sun soaked soil. Our inner kingdom, darkened and infertile by fear, anger, guilt, and an unresolved past that lacks forgiveness, compassion, and love can only provide us, as blinded ones, with a rock strewn ground of unrealized joy and potentiality. Fear, anger, and guilt can only create barren soil.

Do not keep your seed lost in the desert. Awaken your indestructible seed of light so you may feel and know the awakening and growth of all the other seeds intertwined with this little mustard seed of eternal life.

Blessing

In normal times, it is important to pray and bless. During this pandemic, it is even more important to pray and bless. To bless is to acknowledge the divine light within us and in all other things as well as acknowledging and honoring their intrinsic identity and value to the world. When we bless we acknowledge the beauty of the ordinary things of life.

When we bless, we strengthen our relationship to ourselves, to others, and to nature. Bless each day. Give thanks for another day of life to be able to experience the creative opportunities of life.

Bless the sun, the moon, and the rain. Bless the struggle, woundings, and difficulties of life because that is how we grow stronger in our love and light. Bless our loved ones and the strangers we come upon: for this simple act may save a life and the spirit of the one whom we have blessed. Bless with a smile; it is easy.

Bless your food and water; it is the nourishment given to you from the earth and the heavens. Say "thank you" for the simple kindnesses of life. Blessed are the ones who bless with their heart. Blessed are the ones who forgive and learn. Blessed are the ones who are like the babies of the earth. Blessed are the fearless, for they bring light to the darkness. The following are three examples of blessings:

❖ Water: Vital to life but generally taken for granted. "I bless this water of life as it brings joy and vitality to my body. I bless the Earthly Mother and Heavenly Father from whence it came. May it cleanse and purify my inner essence. I say this in a humble and sacred way. So be it."

❖ Meal: "Heavenly Father, Earthly Mother, the Created and the Creator, the All, the One, The Mystery of Mystery, see within my heart. I bless this food and the little ones that gave of their life that our lives may continue. I bless all gathered here. I say this in a humble and sacred way. It is done; so be it."

❖ Night: "I bless this day of life and the life of my loved ones. I bless the ones in pain and need, let them heal. And as I descend into the dreamtime, let love and peace be upon me and my loved ones. The day is done, so be it."

These blessings are given only as guidelines. Moment-to-moment magic of life means that our words of blessing come from our heart at the very moment of the blessing.

The Magic of Breath

Ha me maka ala - Breathe with Conscious Intent

Proper breathing is a simple way to reduce stress and stay in the present moment. Everyone is stressed during this pandemic, especially younger children. Teach your children to breathe consciously and slowly from the "belly" not the chest. Make sure that you are doing the same. In fact, an excellent way to teach them is for you all to do it together. This will calm the body and soothe the soul.

To the Hawaiians the magic of breath is known as *Ha*—breathe out, exhale. The loving essence of the Hawaiian Islands is contained within the concept of the Aloha spirit. Alo means "in the presence of" or "to be with" and *Ha* is "the breath of life." Breath for the Hawaiians symbolizes life as well as the essence of life—the divine. *Ha* is the secret key within aloha. It is the breath that we all share. It is the life-force and consciousness that connects us all. It carries our words, words that may create or destroy throughout the world. To the wise ones of old, words were no less powerful than deeds. One way to experience the presence of the magic of life is to deeply inhale through the nose and softly say *Ha* as you slowly exhale through the mouth. This will help your body and mind relax and be in the present moment.

The word Aloha may be used for healing ourselves. "A" stands for fire, "lo" means to build with proper desire, and "ha." Deeply inhale then exhale "A" (ah), deeply inhale then exhale "lo" (loooo), deeply inhale the exhale "ha" (haaaaaa) blowing the injury, the hurt away. More advanced is to hold your breath after your inhale before verbalizing the exhale. Proper breathing is essential for conducting ritual and ceremony.

Incense

Ritual (a ceremony means more than two people) will propel us into the present moment. It is part and parcel of life and is essential to awakening. Keep a strong mind. Outward and inward distractions will hinder our concentration and will influence and affect the efficacy of ritual. There are three stages to ritual—an opening, the body of the ritual, and a closing. In addition, there are five basic components of what I would call effective sacred ritual:

- ❖ Sacred Mind—refers to our pure intent, focus, and will.

- ❖ Sacred Space—may be as complex as a divine structure (temple or stone circle) or as simple as a place in nature.

- ❖ Sacred Heart—is the opening and closing part of ritual. These are the opening spirit song, prayers, blessings, meditation, acknowledgements, proper attitude, and the compassionate humbleness of the one conducting the ritual.

- ❖ Sacred Words—may be referred to as prayer. Words have power. Blessing or praising is a form of prayer. Each morning we can pray by simply saying: "Greetings to the sun and the earth; I bless this day."

- ❖ Sacred Body—is the act of performing a ritual utilizing movement, sound, sight, and smell. Smells can include the burning of incense or sacred plants.

Incense is important, beneficial, and powerful in many ways. Burning incense puts us in the present moment. Ancient cultures burned different substances that released pleasantly scented smoke. It drifted upwards carrying the prayers and messages of men and women to the gods. The smoke was a physical, psychological, and spiritual link between our seen world and the unseen Otherworld beyond our senses.

Four incenses were especially prized in ancient cultures: frankincense, myrrh, copal, and sandalwood. Frankincense was the most sacred of these ancient incenses. Ancient Greeks used this precious resin as a religious offering. The ancient Egyptians used Frankincense to assist people in manifesting the presence of various gods and as a sign of approval and happiness. Ancient mystics held that these precious scents could stimulate and activate our extrasensory powers and assist use in meditation and during ritual and ceremony.

5. BE GENTLE BUT FIRM

During this pandemic and after, be gentle but firm with yourself in life and in this journey of awakening. As humans we make mistakes and these mistakes sometimes cause pain and suffering to others as well as to ourselves. Life is truly a mystery in its workings; even more mysterious is the pain and suffering it brings to the young and others, who seemingly do not deserve it. From a spiritual philosophical viewpoint, the struggles and sufferings of life are the opportunities for the growth of our spirit. Compassion is needed in our journey to awaken. Always be gentle and compassionate but firm with yourself and be gentle and compassionate with others, especially during this time of our "Great Struggle."

To be gentle but firm is to be like the willow. Do not be an oak tree that fights the wind and breaks but be the willow that bends when it must to the winds of adversity (caused by ourselves, others, or a pandemic), but survives as it forgives the wind and "let's go." Forgiveness is paramount to our spiritual growth. Not forgiveness through a proxy institution, but forgiveness from our heart, of others and of ourselves. Heavenly forgiveness from God is automatic and immediate; you do not need an institution to do this for you.

What is not immediately given is our own earthly forgiveness. The key ingredient here is the letting go of the fear, guilt, shame, anger, and resentment. Sometimes we need to come to the realization that life just happens. We are not being punished for anything.

Be firm with yourself on where you focus most of your attention in life. Is it on money, external power, and always a mindset of "me, me, me," instead of "we, we, we"? Or is it on awakening the light within by being responsible to yourself and others by the caring and compassionate act of wearing a mask and social distancing; an attitude of "me" and "we"?

Focus

Wherever we focus our attention, it receives the greatest amount of our energy for manifestation. Our mind determines our present reality and directly affects our body. "The eye[169] is the lamp of the body. So, if your eye is healthy, your whole body will be full of light; but if your eye is unhealthy, your whole body will be full of darkness. If then the light in you is darkness, how great is the darkness!"[170] We need to determine for ourselves and discover our own proper focus on balancing our divineness and humanness. In this manner, we will discover a vital essence of our heart and mind. It is a quality of an enlightened society. For us in our journey of awakening, it is the discovery of a life journey where we discover peace within our heart and mind and harmony within ourselves. Most importantly, we need to work for peace and harmony within our communities and society at large. May peace be upon us all at this time of the "Great Struggle".

Peace and Harmony where art thou?

There is only one Earth—at least in our Solar System. Yet, so many people are blind to the realization that they are first and foremost "citizens" of Earth—Human Beings with a divine spark within. It escapes people's mind that we share the earth equally with all other creatures and things of nature. This blindness causes separation as people egotistically identify with their own gender, race, religion, and country as their sole persona. There is no unity of being or thought as each identifies with "their own." This leads to thinking that I am right (our own) and you are wrong (others not like us).

The I'm-right-you're-wrong mentality is not quite the worst case of dualism. With little effort it can morph into a dualism of "us" versus "them." The worst case of "us" versus "them," is the type that can erupt into forms of conflict ranging from murder and police abuse/violence rooted in race to the violence of secular and religious wars.

Wherever there is a consciousness of dualism, there is a mind-set of separation. Where there is separation, there is always the potential for fear and conflict. When we individually separate our hearts from our minds, there is conflict within our souls. When we feel separate from nature, our minds want to either conquer or control.

Inner peace is seldom found with this form of thinking. We are not born with dualistic thinking. So where does it originate? Could it be where we first learned to focus our attention while growing up?

First Attention/Second Attention

Our basic life patterns are based on what I call *first attention*, which is rooted in our dualistic consciousness. You may have heard the expression, "energy flows where attention goes." Repetitive energy flow, a constant focus of our mind and our thoughts, will establish our reality and our beliefs about life - about the Earth, nature, others, and ourselves. It will erect core beliefs about all kinds of things including life, death, and religion. From these core beliefs, our rules of life, assumptions, and our attitudes will be formed. Would it surprise you that most people's religion is their parent/parent's religion—their *first attention*?

Each of us is more of a product of our past than we even realize. Troubling behaviors become ignored or unconscious in our stress-filled, hectic, materialistic lives. In addition, these behaviors are connected to our basic rules of life or belief system. All are a result of our *first attention*. This is where our patterns of life were formed growing up. This pandemic may be the perfect time, to focus on dysfunctional beliefs and behaviors of your *first attention* and replace them with functional and beneficial ones coming from a *second attention*.

An example would be represented by a belief resulting from our *first attention* that made us see the glass "half-empty." Our *second attention*, focusing on optimism and the positive potentialities of life, would then replace the old belief with a new one—the glass is "half-full."

Our reality comes from our mind. First and foremost, to increase our love and power, we need to practice forgiveness and release the past's destructive emotional baggage of resentment, anger, guilt, fear, uncertainty, and doubt. By transforming our *first attention* to a *second attention*, we change our patterns, our rules of life, and our beliefs. Usually the most imbedded *first attention* is fear. The opposite of fear—love. Take a moment and list the *first attentions* that you feel need to be changed to a *second attention*.

* * *

When we see our life from a *second-attention*, we begin developing second-sight. There are two results of this. One is opening our "baby eyes,"[171] one of the three pillars of light of Divine Humanity.

Second, the development of shamanic-sight resulting in the brightening of spirit where we become aware of the vibrant coloration of nature. Things will begin to seem more alive, more colorful; the world takes on a different vibrancy and sheen. And we will begin to see things energetically and in a symbolic manner instead of in a literal way.

To begin achieving this second-sight and to consciously change our *first-attention*, we must have an awareness of who we are, what are our beliefs, and what are our rules of life. An exercise to begin this discovery is to draw a picture of who we are. Words many times can not accurately represent who we are but a drawing that we do of ourselves may provide us with great insight. The next step would be a second drawing of who we will be based on our awakening and establishing new *second-attentions*.

Once you have your drawing, explore your old beliefs, and change the ones that need to be changed; and do the same with your rules of life. After completing these second-sight exercises, compose and implement an action plan to replace your dysfunctional (and possibly destructive) *first-attentions* with functional *second-attentions*.

We all need hope. Keep in mind that this pandemic will transform our culture and society into a more equitable, altruistic, and loving one. Please come out the other-side of this coronavirus transformed as well—an awakened, loving, and powerful divine human being.

Manifesting Peace and Harmony

As we have seen, Divine Humanity is a philosophy of whole systems starting "with the realization that there is unity behind diversity, and that, in the manifest world, unity expresses itself through the differentiated image of multiplicity. This manifestation is controlled by the related principles of Nature, Logos, and Harmony, as seen in the Pythagorean sense."[172]

Logos is a "principle originating in classical Greek thought which refers to a universal divine reason, immanent in nature, yet transcending all oppositions and imperfections in the cosmos and humanity."[173] Logos is evidenced by "two main distinctions - the first dealing with human reason (the rationality in the human mind which seeks to attain universal understanding and harmony), the second with universal intelligence"[174]—Divine Mind/Consciousness.

Our hearts and minds are the essential components in discovering our peace and harmony within and outside us in the multiplicity of things. Our consciousness flows from our heart through our mind—the "sun" of our heart gives light to the "moon" of our mind. If our heart is conflicted and our mind disturbed, there can be no peace within our essence.

The ancient Greeks had a concept named *sôphrosunê*, meaning sound or healthy thinking based on self-knowledge. One translation of *sôphrosunê* is *constantia*, which means being (remaining) incapable of being perturbed, or undisturbed.

How often is your mind disturbed? What hinders your mental tranquility? Esoteric Buddhism refers to mental functions that disturb the mind as "hindering passions." This is not romantic, sexual passion but things of the mind, mental functions such as desire, which is the attachment to pleasant things, anger that causes wrath, ignorance, which produces pride and arrogance regarding oneself as superior to others, doubt and false views such as linear time and separation. The esoteric Buddhists were not alone in their thinking of qualities that inhibit our awakening.

Cicero[175] believed that nothing is as universal as stupidity. The ancient Mesoamerican Maya believed that the soul had five enemies—disease, death, stupidity, arrogance, and fear. According to the *Popol Vuh*, "Stupidity was the greatest vice; its cancerous effects could be seen in all the others. The hallmarks of stupidity were ignorance, a kind of overall dullness of spirit, and a naïve incompetence. In the Maya experience, it was because of stupidity that human beings were both fearful and arrogant. If they pursued their educations they would naturally become humbler, and they would learn that by practicing oneness with God they have nothing to fear from either life or death."[176]

The Light of our Moon

That beautiful bright white light in the darkness of the night sky, not alone but surrounded by the twinkling jewels of heaven, has mesmerized humans since the dawn of time. In its fullness it provides us with comfort in the dark of the night but then again in the newness of its darkness it may bring a disconcerting feeling within the depths of our heart. But on the other hand, this feeling will soon be followed by a lifting up of our spirits as we realize that the moon in its darkness will be reborn—just as we will be reborn. The moon has this feeling of timelessness as it voyages through the night sky. It is a fleeting transformative but eternal guardian of nature.

The moon is not solely in the night sky. Within ourselves, we have the light of our own moon. The moon symbolizes our mind while the sun stands for our heart. Symbolically stupidity, ignorance, arrogance, jealousy, and fear may be likened to dark clouds obscuring the light of our moon or as dust on the mirror of our minds. As we all know the moon has no intrinsic light of its own, its light reflects the sun's light. A clean pure mirror reflects a true image, no matter the composite of the image. A dusty mirror (of our mind) obstructs the clarity of our mind. Common sense would indicate that a smoky or dusty mirror can only reflect a distorted image.

Compassion

Compassion is of the heart and gives insight into the transformational power of divine love. Compassion is oneness with the suffering of another. It is a heartfelt connection of self to other. In fact, it lessens the distance or the gulf of separation between self and other. Compassion is a great round mirror of the heart and mind that perceives self and others not as distinctly separate, but as merged identities. The less separate we feel, the more compassionate we can be. But it must be a known faction within one's own life before compassion can be truly felt within the body and heart and not just as a word bandied about for egocentric acceptance.

Compassion flows from the well-spring of self to others when we acknowledge and recognize equality, unity, and our connection to all things. Can a person truly feel and act compassionate when they view themselves as superior to others and the ones suffering? Are their supposed acts conditional or unconditional?

Understanding and being empathic about another's pain and suffering is paramount to our awakening, spiritual growth, and the blossoming of our heart as a flower. To utterly understand compassion, we must believe that everything in creation is connected in a web of divine love. We are all one and no matter what, we are still each other's brother and sister. This Oneness is the greatest jewel, the brightest and clearest diamond of the heavens and the earth. By removing ourselves from fear and anger, our eyes and mind will clear, and our spirit will soar as we express compassion from the depths of our heart.

We all have a story, especially during this pandemic. A story that blends a wondrous tale of light and joy but also a life of darkness, struggle, and suffering. Never judge another for you probably do not know, in totality, their life's story. Never lose sight that we are all each other's brother and sister. A loving and compassionate smile lights up the heavens and may provide someone with the trust and courage that they need; and maybe, just maybe, it might even be enough for this dear one to see some light in the darkness of their life. Help others that are less fortunate. Kindness equates happiness. This virus does not discriminate as humans tend to do. We are all in this together, be kind, caring, and respect each other.

Forgiveness

Forgiveness is greatly misunderstood. Forgiveness is a true release. It is healing the past in the present and is probably the most important attribute to learn as a "pattern of being" for a loving heart. Forgiveness is a cornerstone of awakening. Without forgiveness, we are attached to the past and to others from our past in a dysfunctional manner. We are attached to the past, which becomes our present and potentially, our future. We are "becoming" more distrustful, angry, greedy, and fearful. As a result, it is most difficult to achieve a pure unattached mind in the present. One of the secrets to achieving an unattached mind is forgiveness.

Forgiveness is not forgetting the past, but it is letting go of the attachments to the past. Forgiveness does not give license to our behaviors or the behaviors of others from our past. It does provide us with lessons from the past of the unwanted patterns of conduct of others and ourselves. Forgiveness allows us to learn from the past and provides us with the strength in the moment to help us stop repeating unhealthy patterns of behavior.

Forgiveness is the soothing sun after a bitterly long cold night. It helps us let go of our anger, resentment, doubt, and our guilt, shame, and greed. These are the emotions that generate great energy within us. If not released, they may well mutate into disease and mental imbalance. Using your imagination, visualize a swirling mass of energy that is an emotion, such as anger not released that becomes wrath or revenge. Visual it somewhere within your body, not your mind, but your body. How would this feel? How would this anger/wrath/revenge affect other parts of your body? How would this anger affect your mind, your heart? Now visualize this anger continuing to swirl, but the mind is no longer focused on it. In other words, it is buried while becoming wrath and/or revenge. Now visualize what happens to this energy. Does it change form and harden into a mass? Does it affect nearby cells and organs of the body? If it is still there and not released, it will eventually affect the body adversely.

Metaphorically, this unreleased emotional mass is a *stone*. This *stone,* and others like it, burden us by forming armor and "bodies on our back" that we carry as a part of our being. According to Hawaiian spirituality, these *stones* symbolically reside in our "bowl of light."[177] This is the container of our spirit, our soul—the light that is immortal. These various *stones* dim or suppress the light of our spirit.

Accordingly, our "bowl of light" is a landmark; a symbol of the way back home - back to our oneness of being. According to native Hawaiians, "each child born has at birth, a Bowl of perfect Light. If he tends his Light it will grow in strength and he can do all things - swim with the shark, fly with the birds, know and understand all things. If, however, he becomes envious or jealous he drops a stone into his Bowl of Light and some of the Light goes out. Light and the stone cannot hold the same space. If he continues to put stones in the Bowl of Light, the Light will go out and he will become a stone. If at any time he tires of being a stone, all he needs to do is turn the bowl upside down and the stones will fall away, and the Light will grow once more."[178]

Dropping the *Stone*[179]

"Dropping the *stone*" is a process that is both manifest and visceral for healing our internal wounds. A few of our *stones* may indeed be boulders. To begin healing, we need to choose a more recent wounding; one that is not too large. We want to begin with a small stone, not a large boulder from our distant past. The boulders take time to release. This is the reasoning behind the need for patience and persistence.

To awaken we must not deny emotions. If we deny emotions, especially the challenging ones, we deny our humanness. Each stone may be linked to one or more emotions such as fear or guilt. Keep in mind that emotions are not absolute conditions where you will never again experience them in life such as anger or fear. The key is not to stay attached to them or deny that they exist.

Once the wounding is identified, it is time to "drop the *stone*." Our experiential exercise is conducted in the following manner:

❖ Focus your intent and will on forgiveness of the wounding (issue/emotion) to be released.

❖ Find a *stone* in nature and ask permission with your mind or voice to use it. If yes, take the *stone* and sit with it (preferably in nature) and talk your feelings and emotions—cry/shout/yell, whatever it takes, into this *stone*. You may only spend a few minutes doing this; then put the *stone* away in a special place or you may even carry it with you.

❖ When you are ready to say more words of healing to the *stone*, repeat as often as necessary. This process may take hours, days, weeks, or months (depending on the size of the *stone*). But when you feel ready to release, visit a stream/lake/ocean. It can be at any time of the day, but first light/dawn is best.

❖ Sit by the water's edge and relax. More words may need to be said and more tears shed; when you are ready: Let Go, Forgive, and Release—drop (or toss) the *stone* into the stream/lake/ocean…as you let go of the *stone*—you are letting go of the *stone*, the wounding within your bowl of light. If you are unable to open your fingers and release the *stone*, it just means that you have more work to do on this wounding. Keep this *stone* and take it back home again. Repeat talking to your *stone*. When you feel you are ready again, re-visit the stream/lake/ocean and release. When you have forgiven and let go of this past wounding, sit by the water's edge and feel the lightness within you. Bless the experience… the place, give thanks, and leave an offering before you depart. Bless, thank, and love yourself for having the courage, wisdom, and love to forgive and let go.[180]

Kalehuamakanoelulu'unona pali

Kalehuamakanoelulu'unonapali is the Hawaiian name of Margaret Machado, Auntie Margaret, given to her by her grandfather before she was born. She was the one that carried on her family's tradition of *lomilomi*, traditional Hawaiian massage. Auntie Margaret, who reminded me of my grandmother, was the only authentic Hawaiian kupuna licensed by the state of Hawaii to train therapists in *lomilomi*. She was one of the few people who got away with calling me Jimmy. I chuckled to myself as I recalled her strong hands as she poked my jaw at the hinge point.

"That hurt," I said, wincing in pain.

"Of course, Jimmy," she replied. "You're holding your stress there."

* * *

Auntie Margaret believed in love and forgiveness. She would tell her students, "when you go out to pick herbs, pray; when you prepare them, pray; when you give them, pray. Your patient going to get well.

"And the secret part of it is that before the sun goes down you *ho'oponopono*, you search your heart. *Ho'oponopono* meaning we empty all ourselves and ask for forgiveness before the sun goes down. You can't go to sleep with a troubled mind or troubled heart. You feel good because you're open minded."[181]

Daily Thanks and Forgiveness

Dropping stones will help us forgive the past. How about the present? We do not want to continue to fill our bowl of light with more stones. Additionally, we need to give thanks for all that we have and the love and life of family and friends, the Divine and Mother Earth. During and after this pandemic consider meditating and doing prayers twice a day: once in the morning to give thanks to the source, once in the evening before the sun goes down asking for forgiveness. This cleanses your life daily and nurtures a reverence for life.[182]

6. NOTHING IN EXCESS: MEDEN AGAN

Our next two steps are maxims that were inscribed in the Temple of Apollo at the ancient oracle site of Delphi, Greece. Both are part of the Epsilon (E) of Delphi, meaning divine breath. It is also related to solar rituals, initiations, and our relationship to "light." It is our perpetual relationship with light, the perfection indicating our luminosity—our luminous body, our awakened divine fire. This is our divine fire where the light of knowledge and the warmth of our heart are united.

Usually the accepted consensus is that indigenous cultures of the past worshiped the sun and moon as the primary deities. But that was not the case. Worship of the lord of light, sometimes known as the "Sun behind the sun" predates the worship of the sun and moon. This was, and is, Apollo.

By sight and light, we see and learn. Nothing, therefore, is more natural than to attribute to the light-god the early progress in the arts of domestic and social life. Thus, light came to be personified as the embodiment of culture and knowledge, of wisdom, and of the peace and prosperity which are necessary for the growth of learning.[183]

* * *

Nothing in Excess, attributed to Chilon of Sparta, 6th century BCE, is based on the Greek "*sôphrosunê*, which means moderation, self-control, soundness of mind, and the *harmonia* (well-balanced integration) of the soul."[184]

Sôphrosunê is a multifunctional concept coming together to form the ideal character, it is having self-control, self-knowledge, forethought; it is having temperance, being slow to anger, having restraint, having reason. It also means sound and healthy thinking enabling us to live in accordance with nature. Altogether, they create a life of harmony, peace, and happiness.

There is an association between *sôphrosunê* and our health of body, mind, and spirit. But *sôphrosunê* is also characterized by tension such as between "hubris and the meden agan." Hubris, according to one of the Delphic maxims, is a human's "own self-destructiveness which is produced by a deluded and deviant mind."[185] *Sôphrosunê* is "itself a tightly drawn intermediary between too much and too little."[186]

As we can see, *sôphrosunê* needs itself a measure and must be moderated itself. In other words, temperance is needed. This is not the temperance of restraint and moderation as it is "far from being a reducing kind of moderation but is rather the quality that enables one to get the right mixture or the right balance."[187]

According to Socrates, "the cardinal virtues (wisdom, moderation, justice, courage, and piety) are on the deepest level one. Each of these is understood in terms of a psychic condition participating in the Good: the soul's participation in the Good with respect to knowledge, wisdom; with respect to the gods, piety; with respect to what is to be dared and dreaded, courage; and with respect both to oneself and one's position in relation to others, *sôphrosunê* (moderation). Justice in the individual is participation in the Good through the performance of its proper functions of each part of one's inner self and in society through the performance of his or her proper functions by each agent within society. Wisdom, justice, and *sôphrosunê* blend together to have as their joint consequence courage and piety. One recognizes and accepts oneself: one's abilities, one's nature, one's position in society, one's role. Greed, lust, overweening ambition, including any consuming passion[188] is incompatible with *sôphrosunê*. **Sôphrosunê** is called for in the famous Greek admonitions, 'Know thyself.'"[189] Once again we see the importance of our first step "Know Thyself."

Zeno of Elea, a pre-Socratic Greek philosopher, felt that all pathos was an irrational movement of the soul, an "excessive impulse," which must simply be removed from the soul of the wise man The passions in question were chiefly four: desire, fear, grief, and pleasure. Contrary to Zeno, it is not the removal that is necessary but the moderation, the balance of them in relation to our heart and mind.[190]

According to Epicurus, 341-270 BCE, Ancient Greek philosopher, "the just man is most free from disturbance, while the unjust is full of the utmost disturbance." In the wisdom of Epicurus, list and ponder your passions such as fear and resentment to name a few. Measure them and then develop an action plan to moderate them so that they do not disturb the peacefulness of your mind.

The Peacefulness of our Sanctuary. Photo by Sher.

Cicero suggests four different translations of *sôphrosunê*, that each have their own connotations: *moderatio*, which means moderation in the sense of control and restrain; *constantia*, which means being (remaining) incapable of being perturbed, or undisturbed; *frugalitas*, which means frugality and thrift; and fourth, the most influential: *temperantia*, which means of course temperance. But temperance has in Latin, certainly in Cicero's Latin, the connotation of: "the right mixture", the right balance; *temperare* means to mix different liquids in the right proportion. Concerning temperance, the fundamental idea is the blending of opposites "to achieve a harmonious state, the proper mixture, the *solution*, which frees us to see the right way. In action it is finding the middle way, taking the right action (which may be inaction)."[191]

"The temperate person is one who consistently exercises the 'mean'—the right path between opposite extremes."[192] As we can see, temperance is not restriction but the harmonization of opposites. Its foundation is self-knowledge (*gnóthi seautón*). We are all familiar with a physical sign of temperance—rainbow. The rainbow is an amalgamation of light – a perfect harmonic combination symbolic of life, divinity, promise, harmony, and renewal. The rainbow also symbolizes the androgynous blending of opposites (fire and water). This blending of androgyny is a conjunction of the human and the divine.

Simplify

The idea of moderation led the Greeks to dedicate the greater share of glory and opulence to the divine and the common welfare, rather than keep it for their own private use. This is a far distance from the present mindsets of the wealthy and others. They have no consciousness of a simple lifestyle. According to another Delphic maxim, Become Simple, the wiser a person the simpler they are.

During and after this pandemic, simplify your life and home. "Pretentiousness, ignorance, and bigotry always clothe themselves in the mantle of pomp and hide behind an obscure pseudo-eloquence which hardly anyone can understand. A simple man is a man who lets his actions speak louder than his words… A simple man is also a free man. His wants and needs are small therefore he must not constantly toil to satisfy them. He cannot be tempted or bought easily by material wealth since he has no excessive need for it."[193]

Harmonia

Nothing in Excess includes the concept of *harmonia,* represented by Orpheus' lyre[194]—both important Pythagorean principles. "The central focus of Pythagorean thought is in many respects placed on the principle of *harmonia.* The Universe is One, but the phenomenal realm is a differentiated image of this unity—the world is a unity in multiplicity. What maintains the unity of the whole, even though it consists of many parts, is the hierarchical principle of harmony, the *logos* of relation, which enables every part to have its place in the fabric of the all."[195]

Another meaning of *harmonia* entails "any union in which the parts form a seamless whole while retaining their distinct identities. Harmonia is the daughter of sea-born Aphrodite and fiery Ares, whom Empedocles[196] identified with Love and Strife, the two primary cosmic forces, which bring about all change in the universe. Pythagoras likewise said that cosmic Harmonia is born of the union of Love and Strife. She reconciles all oppositions."[197]

"Love and Strife" is an excellent description of life. Search your heart to see if this is truth. If this is your truth, then follow the maxim of Nothing in Excess and strive to heal the wounds of Strife and fill the spaces of your soul, those that have been left vacant, with Love.

7. KEEP THE MEASURE, RIGHT MEASURE: METRON ARISTON

Observe due measure, for right timing is in all things the most important factor.

— Hesiod, 7th cent. BC, Ancient Greek poet

Ancient knowledge and wisdom never die. The echo of ancient knowledge needs to be heard once again. One small segment of ancient Greek knowledge is connected to ancient Delphi. It is the Delphic maxim "keep the measure." There are a multitude of meanings and teachings connected with this maxim. One meaning is "measure everything before you act," another one: "everything measure excellent" — "right measure." Most importantly, this maxim, right measure – right proportion, goes with self-knowledge. Once again, Know Thyself, our first step.

Ancient cultures believed in the inherent wisdom found in numbers, forms, and ratios. According to the Pythagoreans, "Number was not regarded as an abstract quantity but as the intrinsic and active virtue of the supreme One, of God the source of universal harmony. The science of numbers was that of the living forces, of the divine faculties in action in the universe and in man, in the macrocosm and in the microcosm."[198]

According to Philolaus, the Pythagorean, "Essence in itself escapes man. He knows only the things of this world in which the finite combines with the infinite. And how can he know them? for between things and himself there is a harmony and relation, a common principle; and this principle is given them by the One who gives to them along with their very essence, measure, and intelligibility. It is the common measure between subject and object...."[199]

Keep the Measure may be traced to Apollo himself as he was the god of measure, science, philosophy, and the higher intellectual activities. It refers to the interpenetrative unity of the diversity of creation.

To awaken we need to live this Ancient Philosophy of Keep the Measure or accept due measure (relationship: relation of one thing to another). *Metron Ariston* comes from Pythagorean's mathematicians pointing us to everything in moderation and all in good measure— and all in good time. In other words, moderation (balance) is best, which implies the avoidance of extremes in the lives of human beings. It expresses the pursuit of the Golden Mean and Harmony in most human activities. It is wise advice to measure anything before we act; always measure perfectly.

This Delphic maxim is attributed to *Cleobulus* of Rhodes, one of the seven sages of Greece. Ancient Greeks strongly believed that you should live your life choosing the mean and avoid the extremes on either side, as much as possible. We need to embrace moderation and good measure as well as the Divine Proportion (Golden Mean) in our life and activities.

Divine Proportion

Divine Proportion is a universal symbol for perfection and beauty. The Divine Proportion's importance is revealed by its many names: Golden Mean, Golden Proportion, Golden Section, and Golden Ratio. It's knowledge essential for our Seventh Step. We need to *know ourselves in true proportion*, which emphasizes the intimate connection between our first and seventh and seventh and first steps. In other words, the measure that must be kept is known within—self-knowledge (*gnóthi seautón*). Without *gnóthi seautón* we cannot know our measure. And not knowing, we are unable to "keep" the right measure.

"All these descriptions refer to the proportion that is mathematically described as (Phi). Simply described, it is the relation, in perfect proportion, of the whole to its parts. It is a relationship so perfect that its parts are to each other as the whole is to its larger part."[200] Phi is an irrational and a transcendental number i.e. 1.618034 endlessly repeating.[201] It reveals itself in the world of nature, associated with *phyllotaxis* (Greek for "leaf arrangement."), with the patterns of florets in flowers, with the shape of the nautilus shell and with other natural objects.

Phi reveals and molds the majestic beauty of life. It is through the "Eye of Phi how we find the way between the spaces, through the forces of polarity in the dualistic world of space and time. Phi is unconditional acceptance of all experience, holding no resistance, and passing no judgment, seeing only beauty to become. Phi seeks not to amass, but always gives more than it takes, because phi is not a division of equality but of perfection—the harmonious path (proportion) of love and compassion. Phi is 5 plus Love (1) divided by the relationship of 2; thus, phi is the way, the answer for two—a relationship of compassion and unconditional love."[202] A question to ask ourselves: "what are we becoming by journeying through the seven steps?" and "what will we be after the pandemic (focus on love not fear)?"

* * *

We discover the Divine Proportion in Nature through the Golden Spiral and the Fibonacci sequence of numbers. The Golden Spiral is based upon the Divine Proportion. Mathematically, it is called a "logarithmic spiral. Its growth is as perfect as all other aspects of Divine Proportion, for embedded in this spiral are all the beautiful mysteries of phi's harmony and balance. Intrinsic to its pattern of growth or decay is the perfect ration that says the whole is to the larger as the larger is to the smaller."[203] We discover this spiral in our ear, the human embryo, and even in our DNA.

"If you can't measure it, it doesn't exist"

The ancient Greeks were characterized by their talent for measure, which was primarily aesthetic related to beauty and style found in music and visual arts. Measure is never absolute but a measure of proportion, which means that it is neither the same for everyone nor identical in every circumstance. Measure was based on self-knowledge and, as we have seen, associated with Apollo.

Wherever we find Apollo, we uncover the presence of Dionysus. Apollo the divine aspect while Dionysus is our humanness points us to a *"continuing struggle between the two*, or in other words: from the right proportion between the two that kept them in balance and that maintained their struggle: 'Not in the replacement of intoxication with temperance, but in their placement side by side, lies the Dionysian artistry.'"[204] Our Apollonian measure must be in balance with our Dionysian. In other words, our human artistry is balancing with the right measure of our divineness with our humanness. This is esoteric wisdom.

Apollo cannot exist without Dionysus. The chaotic nature of Dionysus is counterbalanced by the unity and order of Apollo. But there is struggle in balance. A struggle or tension between the spiritual and the physical. Our lives are the story of the contest and interplay between these two, as we struggle to balance and reconcile our physical needs and desires with our spiritual aspirations, our self-focused drives with our altruistic yearnings.

Balance

Keep the Measure relates to the relationship of self (subject) to other (object) with the primary one being microcosm (Relative) to Macrocosm (Absolute). It is the realization that we are "Perfect in our Imperfections which make us Perfect."[205] Additionally, it is knowing the measure of our feelings and the knowledge of people. Once we awaken our spark within, we live the measure of all things by keeping the proper measure and relationship between us and all other things. In other words, "keep the balance." By knowing and living our divineness and by recognizing the divine spark (the Absolute) within the Relative of creation (terrestrial and celestial Mother Nature), we live a balanced state of being.

Most importantly according to the Pythagoreans, "knowledge itself is the third, harmonic element which conjoins the two poles of subject and object. Knowledge then is unifying, much like the harmonic ratios of the musical scale."[206] Direct knowledge is most important and the experience of this knowledge, more than once, results in wisdom.

Skalalitude:[207] *being in harmony with nature - a harmonious state of heart and mind where all things are in balance.*

We may observe and learn from nature where a fundamental axiom is equilibrium, or how forces of nature always seek to balance themselves. Once again, we see the importance of nature, and our relationship to it, in our awakening.

This concept of "keeping the balance" is not limited to the Greeks. There is a Hawaiian concept called *pono*. It refers to a balanced state of mind and heart—harmony. *Pono* also means being in balance with others, nature, and the spirit world. Illness comes from losing our natural state of *pono*. Restoring balance and harmony restores health. Speaking, thinking, and acting properly are the keys to wellness and maintaining *pono*. In totality, "if it is good, if it is in balance, if it is right, if it helps, if it is righteous, if it corrects, if it is responsible, if it is caring, if it honors, if it is humble, if it is peaceful, if it is neat, if it is proper and if it is well mannered, it is *pono*."[208]

Additionally, *pono* was essential in maintaining a state of wellness. "Out of the mating of Wākea [Sky Father] and Papa Honua [Earth Mother], came and continues to come everything in our cosmos, and that's why we're all related and why everything is conscious and communicating. That's the basis for wellness—this constant interaction between all life forces. When there's proper interaction, things are *pono* [balanced]; there's appropriate *mana*, special kind of power or energy maintaining this balance. These spiritual inter-relationships are primary. Proper thoughts and actions maintain this *pono*, harmony."[209]

Keeping ourselves and our relations (all other things) balanced and in harmony (*pono*) is essential for us in our journey of awakening.

Wisdom is the best of all things; ignorance is the worst.
— Plato

Our concept of self and other is best represented by the measure of love in human relations: You shall love your neighbor as yourself. When we have a knowing within our hearts that we have starlight, a "spark of creation—a sun of God," within us and a knowing that others do also, we are then able to truly "love our neighbor," to forgive, and to have compassion for others. This is the heart knowledge of the oneness of life and the heart knowledge of the humanness, the joy, the struggles, and the suffering of life. We understand our own selves, and we understand others. This is true empathy and compassion.

Our balanced state of being is not static and is based on our self-measure, which needs to be open to growth and self-mastery. We must discover the mean or balance between too little and too much. For instance, "rainfall may vary in space-time, as regards to intensity and duration, but is neither too much (to the extent that all life on earth is flooded off to total extinction) nor too little (to the extent that no life on earth can be sustained)."[210]

To summarize: Apollo (Divine) and Dionysus (Human—all things). Before we awaken, we must discover the right proportion between our spiritual focus and our material focus. And once awakened, we must discover the right proportion between Apollo and Dionysus not as a static proportion but one that we strengthen. Accordingly, the value of our measure in awakening and once awakened is the extent to which we manage to grow in our balance of our divineness and humanness. Once our divine fire/spark is awakened, with the right measure, we strengthen it, strengthen our luminosity—our luminous body. According to Pre-Columbian Nahuatl Philosophy: The wise man is a light, a torch, a stout torch that does not smoke. Once awakened. We achieve the *resurrection body* or a light luminous body—the miracle of turning death into resurrection.

Measurelessness

Corresponding to the ancient Delphic Pythagorean maxim, it is wise advice to measure anything before we act; always measure perfectly. As we can see from the lack of measure, our culture and society are measureless. The dysfunction of being measureless results in hubris, exaggerated self-pride, this recklessness goes hand in hand with *atē*,[211] being blinded. *Atē* was the ancient Greek personified spirit of delusion, infatuation, blind folly, rash action, and reckless impulse who led people down the path of ruin.

The lack of measure, or "measurelessness", as well results in holding onto rigid and dogmatic measures, such as the Church deeming abortion a sin. Christianity desires to control, stupefy, and intoxicate with fear; the one thing it does not desire is measure. The 2020 pandemic glaringly exposed the measurelessness of our culture and society.

Of this maxim it has been said that the ancient Greek Seven Sages wished humankind to observe due measure and proportion in all matters instead of making irrevocable decisions about any human affairs. It has been obvious that "due measure and proportion" was a far cry from the response to the pandemic due to the hubris, exaggerated self-pride, recklessness, self-centeredness, narcissistic and egocentric personality of the President and his cronies.

When we are unauthentic in "who we are," we are on the verge of being measureless. The dysfunction of being measureless results in stupidity, *hubris*, and a recklessness that goes hand in hand with *at* .

What are we Becoming?

Divine Humanity states that spirit (unseen universe) and matter (seen universe) interpenetrate or blend together—a radical nonduality. We would recognize the pairs of opposites but know the blended unity of the All. Once awakened, the key to power and life is the proper or right measure of this blending. Our consciousness would always be aware of spirit, the Otherworld, but our daily focus would be on this world. Once awakened, we will have embraced and become a reflection of the Divine Proportion sometimes referred to as the Golden Section:

The power of the golden section to create harmony arises from its unique capacity to unite different parts of a whole so that each preserves its own identity, and yet blends into the greater pattern of a single whole.[212]
—Gyorgy Doczi, The Power of Limits

All life strives toward phi.
What are we becoming?
(Mathematically) We become Φ (phi)!

Seven Twice

*Seven is the key to the creation of Moses and the symbol of the
entire Jewish religion.*
— Eliphas Lévi

There is one important thread that weaves through our seven
steps. Even though it might not be obvious—balance the key to life
and awakening. Seven twice refers to the number fourteen the total
of our seven steps repeated twice: Step One to Step Seven; Step Seven
back to Step One—Fourteen.

Our resurrection of spirit and awakening is to be found in *nun*,
the fourteenth letter of the Arabic and Hebrew alphabet, with a numerical value of fifty. *Nun* signifies a fish, a whale, which leads us to the
tale of Jonah and the whale.[213] "Jonah's emergence from the belly of
the whale has always been regarded as a symbol of resurrection and
therefore of passage to a new state and this must be compared, on
the other hand, with the idea of 'birth' which, in the Hebrew Kabbala
especially, is attached to the letter nun and which must be understood
spiritually as a 'new birth', that is, a regeneration of the being, individual or cosmic."[214]

* * *

Within the mysteries of the original tarot, known as
"Philosophical Medicine,"[215] the fourteenth card of the tarot is Balance
or Temperance.[216] The Hebrew letter for this card is *nun*. In ancient
Hebrew, *nun* is a picture of a seed sprout—new generation. Nun
alludes to the name Immanuel meaning "God in us."

This card's numerical value is fifty. It is a card of blending of
the metaphoric fire and water—a place of balance. It is the card of
Aquarius, and it reveals knowledge of the coming Age of Aquarius.
With the value of fifty, it is the divine power of five on a higher plane

of consciousness—ten times five equals fifty. This tarot card portrays the angelic queen of heaven holding an urn in each hand. One urn is golden, and the other urn is silver, symbolizing the spiritual and physical energies within us. The spirit energies reside in the pineal gland, and the physical energies within the sacrum or coccyx. And the meeting point—the heart focused on Love.

The angelic queen is blending the energies together. This card represents the interpenetration of spirit and matter—divine and human. Symbolically, this is where we cleanse "our faulty perceptions, connecting us in a divine yet human way with the immutable world beyond the reach of time's scythe."[217]

Another image of tarot card fourteen illustrates the Archangel Mikaël who is pouring water upon the "lion of fire," and ignites the "eagle of water" with a burning torch. In other words, "burning water" representing the blending of fire (heaven - spirit) and water earth - (material)—radical nonduality.

POSTSCRIPT

Pandemic Storytime: What story are you going to write about "who you are" now; what have you learned from the seven steps and this pandemic, and how have you made yourself better?

APPENDIX

The Four Winds and the Heart of Heaven and Earth Feathered Serpent Medicine Wheel

Gate of Practice – South and West

❖ The Path of Reflection and Forgiveness in the South. Element: Water (Emotions).

❖ The Path of Transformation situated in the West. Element: Earth (Body).

Gate of Awakening – North and East

❖ The Path of Peace, Harmony and Wisdom located from which the North wind blows. Element: Air (Mind).

❖ The Path of Oneness in the East. Element: Fire (Spirit).

The Center of the Medicine Wheel

❖ The Gate of the Heart in the Center—Awakening as a Divine Human – a Feathered Serpent. Element: Space.

Furthermore, each direction is represented by a symbolic animal:

❖ South (emotion): Serpent

❖ West (body): Large Cat such as Jaguar or Lion

❖ North (mind): Hummingbird

❖ East (spirit): Eagle

❖ Center (awakened to radical nonduality): Feathered Serpent

Please contact us if you are interested in joining us and journeying through the medicine wheel as an apprentice and/or on-line classes assisting your journey of awakening: bigcatthatflies@gmail.com, http://www.snowyowlspeaks.info/, http://www.spartanwarrior-philosophers.com/home, http://divinehumanity.com/

Rev. Dr. JC Husfelt and Rev. Sherry Husfelt

Photo by Terri Bellas, July 2019.

JC and Sherry have been referred to as "magicians who are able to take a group of people into the dimensions of their souls – fluid dancers that know where a group needs to go!"

Rev. Dr. JC Husfelt, Philosopher: discipline - metaphysics, which deals with such abstract subjects as cosmology, theology, the nature of being and epistemology, which is the science concerned primarily with the nature of knowledge itself and the question of whether it may exist in an absolute form; master martial artist with fifty plus years of experience; and holder of shamanic lineages and traditions.

In Dr. Husfelt's "other life," he was a teacher and national wellness consultant with clients ranging from L.L. Bean to the United States Senate.

Dr. Husfelt's Books Available on Amazon:

❖ *I Am A Sun Of God And So Are You* (AuthorHouse, 2004): The ancient, yet startlingly simple wisdom at the core of this book has the power to transform the world by uniting spirit and matter. Divinity and humanity.

❖ *The Return of the Feathered Serpent* (AuthorHouse, 2006): In a monumental and epic time of need, the hero reappears. To the Mesoamericans, their returning prophet or cultural hero was known as Quetzalcóatl—the Feathered Serpent.

❖ *Return of a Green Philosophy* (Snowy Owl, 2015): If you seek a deeper level of understanding—and practical, commonsense direction for finding your way toward wisdom— then join Dr. JC Husfelt for an in-depth exploration of the ancient Norse-Germanic tradition—and the tremendous wisdom it offers for living in harmony with nature.

❖ *Do You Like Jesus—Not the Church?* (Snowy Owl, 2015): Bold and revealing, this book offers an opportunity to rethink the complex relationship between Jesus and the self-interested organization whose lies distort Jesus's very nature. Free yourself from the lie and discover the powerful, inclusive, and egalitarian truth that lies beneath—Jesus's true message: the kingdom of God within us and outside us.

❖ *Tequila and Chocolate, The Adventures of the Morning Star and Soulmate - A Memoir* (Snowy Owl, 2019): Think Indiana Jones meets Gandalf the Grey. This book is pure inspiration. It is like sitting down with a shaman, a philosopher, a spiritual master, and a far traveler to have a conversation about the adventures of a reluctant prophet and his soulmate.

ENDNOTES

1   From a sixth century text named the *Shinhinmei* refers to the way of Zen.

2   Attar was a great Persian Sufi mystic who lived in the latter part of the twelfth century.

3   Please see our tale in our memoirs: "Chicken, Candles, and Posh."

4   James E. Brady and Jeremy D. Coltman, "Bats and the Camazotz: Correcting a Century of Mistaken Identity," 232 - 233.

5   https://ancientmayalife.blogspot.com/2018/03/scribes.html

6   The virus most likely came from a bat.

7   Waters, *Mexico Mystique* (Swallow Press/Ohio University Press books, 1975), 224.

8   Malcolm Godwin, *The Holy Grail* (Viking Penguin, 1994), 24.

9   Adapted from http://shorelinedriftwood.blogspot.com/2009/11/understanding-classical-greek-mythology.html

10   Maria Cramer and Mihir Zaveri, "What if You Don't Want to Go Back to the Office?," May 5, 2020, The New York Times.

11   Pali Jae Lee and Koko Willis, *Ho'opono*

12   Brian Clark, "At Home with Hestia: a return to center," May 5, 2020 (https://mountainastrologer.com/tma/at-home-with-hestia-a-return-to-center/)

13   My birth guardian or birth co-essence.

14   Elizabeth Van Buren, *Refuge of the Apocalypse: Doorway into Other Dimensions* (The C.W. Daniel Company Ltd., 1986) 206.

15   Nana Veary, *Change We Must* (Institution of Zen Studies, 1989), 39.

16   Please see Appendix.

17   Paraphrased from Rachmond Howard, *The Zodiac in our Genes*, 18.

18   Excerpted from Manly P Hall, *The Secret Teachings of all Ages* (The Philosophical Research Society, 1977), Introduction.

19   Rev Dr JC Husfelt, *Do You Like Jesus – Not the Church?* (Snowy Owl, 2015), xxxvii.

20   Green refers not only to Divine Humanity being an ecological religion but as well a religion of the heart. Green is the color of the heart chakra. The heart is the balance between heaven and earth energies while green is the mid-point of the color spectrum.

21   Original Divinity: The immediate response that may pass through a person's mind to the religious philosophical principle of original divinity, that we are

born with a divine, indestructible seed of light instead of original sin, takes the form of a question: "Why then do humans make war, kill, rape, and fly planes into buildings?"

The short answer is that the divine spark or seed has not been awakened. Knowing this and the realization that we are still humans with a body, mind, emotion and spirit and we will always have the choice of right-action, wrong action, a combination of both or inaction. In other words, even after we awaken our divineness, we will make human mistakes and possibly do actions that are not true and right. Knowing ourselves means that we will love, and we will fear; we will struggle, and we will overcome; we will suffer, and we will have joy and happiness; we will live, and we will die. This is knowing ourselves and then striving to become more divine with as little human wrong doing as possible.

"In our deepest selves, we are divine. All living things are divine in their deepest selves. Now, that divine self may be hidden or covered over by hatred, envy, fear or other negative things. But, it is there nonetheless, and it is our 'true' and 'eternal' selves." (Husfelt, *Do You Like Jesus – Not the Church?*, 294).

22 "Jesus did not believe in original sin. He believed in original divinity, in purity, as each of us has the spark, the starlight of God, within us." [Ignatius Singer, *The Rival Philosophies of Jesus and of Paul* (Palala Press, 2016) 313 - 314.]

"Judaism does not believe in original sin. Thus, there is no need for a savior in Judaism as there is in Christianity. God's natural, altruistic law, stated in Jeremiah 31:33 that 'it will be written on their hearts,' means that as soon as the soul, the breath and light of God, enters the body at birth, God's divine mandate of love and compassion is written on the heart. The logical conclusion would be that the little one is thus born in divinity and not in sin.

"Jesus was Jewish; as stated above, Judaism does not believe in the existence of original sin but of original purity. (Husfelt, *Do You Like Jesus – Not the Church?*, 65, 209 - 210.)

23 Singer, *The Rival Philosophies of Jesus and of Paul*, 313 - 314

24 Godwin, *The Holy Grail*, 212.

25 In theology, the concept that the world is controlled by two opposing forces, i.e., good and bad, God and Satan. In Philosophy the idea that the world consists of two main components: thought and matter. (http://www.spiritrestoration.org/Theological_Terms/Calvinism_to_Dualism.htm)

Philosophical belief that reality is essentially divided into two distinct kinds of categories. Typically mind and body or the related pair, spirit and matter. One concept in each pair is often deemed superior to the other. (http://www.thegreenfuse.org/glossary.htm)

A form of binary thinking that divides the world into good versus evil with no middle ground tolerated. (http://www.publiceye.org/glossary/glossary_big.html)

The three major western religions, Judaism, Christianity and Islam are based on the separation philosophy of dualism with Christianity emphasizing the dualism represented by God and Satan; good verses evil.

26 "The expression 'Divine spark' can be misleading, as can any metaphysical term taken too literally. The word 'spark' gives an image of a fiery particle thrown away from a central fire. Some have taken this literally, seeing humanity as 'sparks' that originated in the Light, but which have flown out and away from the Source. This view is contrary to the witness of the Sages and the teaching of the Mysteries. The term 'Divine spark' refers to the Immanence of God within each heart. But the Infinite One is not a pie that can be cut into slices. Where the Indivisible One is, at ant single point (or spark) there the All-Holy abides in the fullness (pleroma) of Wisdom and Love and in the plenitude of Divine Power." (David Goddard, *The Tower of Alchemy*, p. 147)

27 "The symbolism of dew, closely connected with that of rain by its very nature, is likewise related more especially to the giving of life; and this symbolism is common to numerous traditional forms—Hermetism, the Hebrew Kabbala, and to the Far Eastern tradition" (Rene Guenon, *Fundamental Symbols*, 246)

28 I use various symbolic words to describe the fragment of God or the Absolute within us as purely written or spoken words alone are inadequate to express the Absolute. "There is no question about the affability of our word of reality, for we communicate with each other about the various phenomena which occur in this world by means of language. But when it comes to the absolute realm, the world of enlightenment, language is no longer a suitable mode of expression.... on the other hand, the realm of the absolute is also expressible, although not of course by means of the written or spoken word, but through symbols. (*Mikkyo Kobo Daishi Kukai and Shingon Buddhism*, p. 34)

29 "No one after lighting a lamp puts it under the bushel basket, but on the lampstand, and it gives light to all in the house. In the same way, let your light shine before others so that they may see your good works...." (*Matthew, 5: 15 - 16*)

30 Dennis Overbye, "American and 2 Japanese Physicists Share Nobel for Work on LED Lights," October 7, 2014, http://www.nytimes.com/2014/10/08/science/isamu-akasaki-hiroshi-amano-and-shuji-nakamura-awarded-thenobel-prize-in-physics.html?_r=0.

31 A fabulous precious blue stone believed to cause the phoenix to renew her youth. According to Wolfram von Eschenbach, the lapis exilis was synonymous with the Holy Grail.

32 Anna Morduch, *The Sovereign Adventure: The Grail of Mankind* (James Clark, 1970), 31.

33 Sherry and I have conducted these shamanic resurrection rituals. Our stories are told within our memoirs—*Tequila and Chocolate*.

34 For the complete true message of Jesus and not the lie of Christianity, please see my book: *Do You Like Jesus—Not the Church? Jesus: His True Message - Not the Lie of Christianity*.

35   Morduch, *The Sovereign Adventure: The Grail of Mankind*, 162.

36   "I believe in Spinoza's God, who reveals himself in the lawful harmony of the world," he told him, "not in a God who concerns himself with the fate and the doings of mankind." Albert Einstein

37   Our conscious mind is usually based on dualism, not a radical nondualistic consciousness. For the majority of people, their worldview is dualism – separation of the binaries such as male and female, spirit and matter, the brain's right hemisphere and the brain's left hemisphere. And politically, Democrat and Republican. Take a moment and

ponder how this consciousness feeds the fires and flames of tribalism, sexism, and racism to name just a few resulting from a mindset of dualism.

38   Reproductive Justice is the human right to maintain personal bodily autonomy, have children, not have children, and parent the children we have in safe and sustainable communities. It also includes the right to control birthing options, right to affordable health care, and the right to comprehensive sex education

39   Hall, *The Secret Teachings of All Ages*, 15.

40   Based on the extraordinary ontological opus of the physicist David Bohm (1917 – 1992), a colleague of Albert Einstein: "In sum, Bohm's model of reality consists of a dynamic holomovement (this is similar to my ontological theory that the un-manifest, Great Mystery Absolute Reflected itself to manifest Creation) that has three basic realms or levels of manifestation: the explicate order, the implicate order, and the superimplicate order–with the latter two realms constituting the bulk of reality. (River of Truth by Will Keepin posted online by Alex Paterson:

http://www.vision.net.au/~apaterson/science/david_bohm.htm#-SCIENCE%20AND%20SPIRIT)

41   Hawaiian Shaman-Priests

42   David Kaonohiokaala Bray, *The Kahuna Religion of Hawaii*, 24

43   https://www.technologyreview.com/s/612844/what-is-quantum-computing/

44   Laurette Séjourné, *Burning Water* (Shambhala, 1976), Introduction, 99.

45   Ibid, 99.

46   Passions are anything that disrupts the tranquility of the mind. The five basic passions are: desire, anger, stupidity-ignorance, pride-arrogance, and doubt.

47   http://www.rosetta.bham.ac.uk/issue6/pythagoras-sparta/

48   David Fideler, *Jesus Christ Sun of God: Ancient Cosmology and Early Christian Symbolism* (Quest Books, 1993), 23.

49   Athon Veggi and Alison Davidson, *The Book of Doors*, 13.

50   Ibid., 11.

51   Husfelt, *Do You Like Jesus – Not the Church?*, 8 - 9.

52   This is appropriate when you consider that I am the Morning Star. Venus as the morning star rises in the darkest part of the night and is seen by only a few

who are awake (awakened) at a time when the majority of the world is asleep. Thus, Venus, in its morning-star cycle, is like the thief in the night as it is noticed by only a few. The name morning star in the original Hebrew and Arabic meant "that which comes in the night or one who knocks at the door."

53 *Pseudo Dionysus: The Classics of Western Spirituality* (Paulist Press, N.Y.), 152.

54 Ritualistic immersion in running water (a stream or river) or the ocean is one of the oldest forms of initiation and symbolic death and rebirth. It is one of the essential steps in awakening, frightening but necessary. We need to symbolically "die" to the old to be "born again" – our second birth. Furthermore, this second birth may be referred to as a "virgin birth." As we can see, it is not membership in an earthly or religious institution. It is the beginning of an awakening to the truth of the world and one's authentic self.

Few in the world still practice and teach this form of purification. Even in Jesus's time, baptism in the River Jordan was a "unique event that even Catholic editors of the Jerusalem Bible consider to be an initiation." Outside of the Mandeans of the Middle East, the greatest concentration of "dawn bathers" is to be found within the indigenous communities that still practice and adhere to the old ways. But even here, there are few still alive that can "initiate" and put people into the "living waters" of the Earth.

Sher and I are blessed to be two of those who still practice and "initiate" people into bathing. This "initiation" is not one of membership, but one of death and resurrection/rebirth.

Bathing is always begun pre-dawn. In the predawn time, the darkness is always thickest. The air brings a pleasant freshness awaiting the return of light. Imagine standing nude before first light on the edge of a flowing river while listening to the sounds of the rushing, roaring waters as if they are the sounds of a thundering heavenly chariot. This is the coldest time of the night, at first light right before dawn. It is the liminal time between dark and light. A magical moment reflecting our mortality and, most importantly, our immortality.

And further imagine your bare feet on the sacred ground of the Earth (sometimes snow-covered), your naked body feeling the winds of the Earth while your uncovered head and eyes observe the dimming night sky, one embedded with hundreds of sparkling jewels. And then you voice prayers before entering the water alone and submerging yourself. When I enter the river, with my first step, there is an explosion of my senses and dualistic reality dissolves into a oneness of truth. With my first squatting submersion, I die once again, only to be reborn as I explode straight up out of the water, into the air. A primal scream escapes my lips as the icy fire of spirit exploded through me in a wild, ecstatic rush—molten fire blended with liquid ice. And for a split second, my mind shifts into the realization that I must do this three more times.

As I exit the river, the dark of night has given way and brought the dawn-first light. (Husfelt, *Tequila and Chocolate*, 190, 195.)

55 There is no greater external sign of the Holy Spirit of God than the morning star, the planet Venus, which symbolizes rebirth in Judaism. Even the historical geographical center of Judaism, Jerusalem, is connected with Venus. Its name "effectively means the place dedicated to Venus in its evening setting." [Christopher Knight and

Robert Lomas, Book of Hiram: Freemasonry, Venus, and the Secret Key to the Life of Jesus (Barnes & Noble, 2005) 84.]

56 Please see the story in our memoirs: "Spirit Man of Teotihuacán," where I'm identified as *Quetzalcóatl*.

57 Malcolm Godwin, *Angels: An Endangered Species* (Simon & Schuster, 1990), 237.

58 According to Gareth Knight, "Archangels are real beings though they have not physical bodies. Their anthropomorphic forms, as represented in religious painting, for example come from the human mind, which has to have a mental form acceptable to the understanding. More appropriate forms would be pillars of vast force… such would be more in accordance with the real 'appearance' an Archangel would assume." The Author Gareth Knight, 90 years old, has spent a lifetime unearthing and teaching the principles of magic as a spiritual discipline and method of self-realization. (Gareth Knight, *A Practical Guide to Qabalistic Symbolism*, 43 – 44.)

59 Paul Broadhurst, *Tintagel and the Arthurian Myths* (Pendragon Press, 1990), 191.

60 Rabbi Julian Sinclair, "Ahavah," The JC.com, October 28, 2008. (https://www.thejc.com/judaism/jewish-words/ahavah-1.57740)

61 Bernard Faure, *Visions of Power: Imagining Medieval Japanese Buddhism* (Princeton University Press, 1996), 16.

62 Priya Hemenway, *Divine Proportion* (Sterling Publishing), 183.

63 Edward F. Malkowski, *The Spiritual Technology of Ancient Egypt*, 125 and the Schwarz Reflection Principle.

64 Fideler, *Jesus Christ Sun of God*, 59 – 60.

65 Hemenway, *Divine Proportion*, 51.

66 F. H. Colson and G. H. Whitaker (trans), *Philo De Opificio Mundi*, vol. 1, 13.

67 Joseph Campbell, *The Hero with a Thousand Faces* (Princeton University Press, Princeton, 1972), 269.

68 Husfelt, *Do You Like Jesus, Not the Church?*, 224.

69 Ibid.

70 Divine mind and consciousness, divine spark in the "dark," divine spark in the "light".

71 Husfelt, *Do You Like Jesus, Not the Church?*, 225.

72   Georg Luck, *Arcana Mundi* (The Johns Hopkins University Press, 1985, 2006), 33.

73   Ibid, 5.

74   Husfelt, *Do you Like Jesus - Not the Church?*, 182.

75   Ibid.

76   Consciousness is fully explained in my book *Do You Like Jesus—Not the Church?*, 216 – 219.

77   Quote from the movie, "The Last Samurai."

78   Morduch, *The Sovereign Adventure*, 108.

79   Excerpted from: https://www.ncbi.nlm.nih.gov/pmc/articles/PMC5442367/

80   Just as humanity in Divine Humanity represents not only the human race but all things of creation, brother or sister means all things of creation.

81   Husfelt's, *Tequila and Chocolate, The Adventures of the Morning Star and Soulmate, A Memoir*, 182.

82   The ancient motto of Husfelt (Scottish-Norse earthly lineage) is "In Time," with the image of an hourglass. The esoteric meaning, birth and rebirth: "The higher and lower vessels represent Heaven and Earth, and the descending sand or fluid represents the stream of spirit descending into matter; it shows us that although the life force runs out, there may be an inversion, a return of the spirit to heaven, and a rebirth." (John Opsopaus, *Pythagorean Tarot*, 130.)

83   Joseph Campbell, *The Mythic Image* (Princeton University Press, Princeton, 1981), 262.

84   Fideler, *Jesus Christ Sun of God*, 134.

85   Ross Nichols, *The Book of Druidry* (Thorsons, Hammersmith, London, 1992), 128

86   Veary, *Change We Must*, 61.

87   Husfelt, *Do you Like Jesus - Not the Church?*, 182.

88   First Knowledge is knowledge that is woven throughout and found in all the first people's spiritual/religious traditions on this earth. This first knowledge has been referred to as primordial knowledge or the Primordial Tradition (perennial philosophy). As such, it portrays universal themes, principles, and truths. In other words, "the term Primordial Tradition is utilized to describe a system of spiritual thought and metaphysical truths that overarches all the other religions and esoteric traditions of humanity." Furthermore, "the perennial philosophy proposes that reality, in the ultimate sense, is One, Whole, and undivided—the omnipresent source of all knowledge and power. We do not perceive this reality because the field of human cognition is restricted by the senses. But the perennial philosophy claims that these limitations can be transcended." (Rev. Dr. JC Husfelt, *Return of a Green Philosophy*, xiii.)

89   Thomas Paxson, http://www.siue.edu/EASTASIA/paxon_102199.htm

90   http://www.theosophy-nw.org/theosnw/human/hu-wtst2.htm

91   Husfelt, *I Am A Sun of God And So Are You*, AuthorHouse, 2004.

92   David Fideler, *The Pythagorean Sourcebook and Library*, (Phanes Press), 33.

93   Ibid, 31.

94   Priya Hemenway, *Divine Proportion*, 66.

95   http://www.theosophy-nw.org/theosnw/human/hu-wtst2.htm

96   Marios Koutsoukos, *Pillars of Humanity*, e-book, 524 - 525.

97   Based on the extraordinary ontological opus of the physicist David Bohm
      (1917 - 1992), a colleague of Albert Einstein, astrology is seen as a valid and
      sacred science. "David Bohm's most significant contribution to science is his
      interpretation of the nature of physical reality, which is rooted in his theo-
      retical investigations, especially quantum theory and relativity theory. Bohm
      postulates that the ultimate nature of physical reality is not a collection of
      separate objects (as it appears to us), but rather it is an undivided whole that is
      in perpetual dynamic flux. For Bohm, the insights of quantum mechanics and
      relativity theory point to a universe that is undivided and in which all parts
      'merge and unite in one totality.' This undivided whole is not static but rather
      in a constant state of flow and change.

"Bohm calls this flow the holomovement – holo, meaning holographic-like,
and movement, suggesting dynamism and process. . .. In other words, the
nature of reality is a single unbroken wholeness in flowing movement. So,
everything is connected, and everything is in dynamic flux. Now, in this
term holomovement, holo refers to holographic structure, meaning that
each part of the flow, in some way, contains the entire flow. . .. And the
movement part of holomovement is that the whole flow is in a continual
process of change.

"Bohm proposes that the holomovement consists of two fundamental
aspects: the explicate order and the implicate order. . .. What we call matter
is merely an apparent manifestation of the explicate order of the holomovement. . .. In other words, the explicate order is the manifest realm; it is the
physical space-time universe in which we live. This explicate order is the
surface appearance of a much greater enfolded or implicate order, most of
which is hidden. Thus, the implicate order is the unseen or the unmanifest
realm.

"It's tempting, perhaps, to think of the explicate order as the primary reality,
and the implicate order as a subtle, secondary reality. For Bohm, precisely
the opposite is the case. The fundamental primary reality is the implicate
order, and the explicate order is but a set of ripples on the surface of the
implicate order. So that which we can see and feel, and touch is merely the
waves on the surface of reality, which is a vast ocean of implicate order. "In
reference to the alchemical axiom of 'as above, so below,' the microcosm has
all the elements, essentially of the macrocosm. It is important to empha-
size that each part does contain the whole, not at a manifest level but at a
process level.

"This all leads to a kind of metaphorical understanding of how astrology might work, and it works in a way that is not mechanistic. This is particularly important to understand. It is not that Pluto (planet) sends rays down to your brain, which acts as a radio receiver, picks them up, and goes and does Plutonic things. And it is not that Pluto is in you, in the sense that the physical Pluto is much too big to be contained in your physical body. It's that the process that's going on in Pluto is also going on in you. Literally. So, Pluto is literally contained in you, and in me, but at the process level, not at the manifest level.

"Astrology, in a sense, is a science of the order in meaning and of its interpenetration with the physical space-time universe. And this is where I think astrology is so profound. Because, in a sense, all of the esoteric sciences, such as the I Ching, Tarot and others, are sciences of the order of meaning. They are essentially models of the implicate order. But what is so profound about astrology is that, by virtue of its connection to planets and stars, it also precisely models the interpenetration between the invisible realms of meaning and the physical space-time universe. So, what do I foresee, or perhaps pray for, for the future of science? Essentially, a grand synthesis of explicate and implicate sciences. Today's orthodox science would come to be seen as a partial science we see all around us and mistakenly take for the whole of reality. Meanwhile, astrology and the other esoteric sciences are sciences of the implicate order, and rather than contradicting the physical sciences, astrology and physics are two aspects of a much greater whole. This will eventually lead to a grand synthesis of sacred and secular sciences into a much more profound science than we have today."
[The preceding is excerpted from two sources: William Keepin, "*The Life-work of David Bohm*," Vision Net, (http://www.vision.net.au/~apaterson/science/david_bohm.htm); and William Keepin, "Astrology and the New Physics: Integrating Sacred and Secular Sciences," The Mountain Astrologer, Oct/Nov 2009.]

98   https://blazinglight.net/2014/10/05/12th-house-planets-hidden-power/

99   "As above, so below" and "As below, so above" is also an ancient Jewish axiom. (http://www.chazonhatorah.org/journey-to-the-secret-city-of-luz-metatron-me-tatron-jacob-s-ladder-to-the-face-of-god.htm)

100   *The Mountain Astrologer*, Oct./Nov. 2008

101   http://thezodiac.com/soul/oracle/whentheoraclespoke.htm

102   Rev. Dr. JC Husfelt, "Natal Fixed Star Report," Zyntara Publications, 2.

103   Explained in our fifth step Be Gentle but Firm.

104   Excerpted from Roberta H. Markman and Peter T. Markman, *Masks of the Spirit* (University of California

Press, 1994), 150.

105   Koutsoukos, *Pillars of Humanity*, e-book, 524 – 525.

106   Joseph Campbell, *The Power of Myth*, (Doubleday, 1988) 5.

107   (http://en.wikipedia.org/wiki/The_Hero_with_a_Thousand_Faces)

108   Unhealthy ego

109   Pali Jae Lee and Koko Willis, Tales from the Night of the Rainbow (Night Rainbow Publishing Co., 1990), 53.

110   I am not motivated or burdened by guilt in this lifetime, but I would discover much later in life that I was carrying great guilt within my heart and soul from a previous lifetime.

111   Husfelt, *Tequila and Chocolate, The Adventures of the Morning Star and Soulmate*, 60.

112   Anything that disturbs the tranquility of the mind/consciousness.

113   This is not the faith of institutional religion.

114   This is not the "faith" of Christianity as at this time in history, there was no such thing as a religion called Christianity. Jesus is talking about the faith within ourselves and faith in the beauty and harmony of nature and creation.

115   Nichols, *The Book of Druidry*, 128

116   Inscription over gateway at Delphi meaning divine breath (Ross Nichols, *The Book of Druidry*, p. 131) In addition, E is pronounced with an "a" sound while A is pronounced as an "au" sound.

117   The Hebrew *Hé* corresponds to the English E-fifth letter.

118   Campbell, *The Power of Myth*, 230 – 231.

119   John Charlot, *Chanting the Universe* (Emphasis International Limited, 1983), 84.

120   Elithe Manuha'a ipo Kahn, Ph.D., *"Ha" Breathe*, (Zen Care, Honolulu, Hawaii), 23.

121   Michael Green, *The Book of the Dragontooth*, 16.

122   Kate Kelland, "Scientists warn of potential wave of COVID-linked brain damage," Science News

      July 7, 2020 (https://www.reuters.com)

123   Pam Gregory, "Buckle up for Mars retrograde in Aries," Mountain Astrologer, June/July 2020, 36 – 38.

124   Manly P. Hall, *The Secret Teachings of all Ages*, 11.

125   The Gospel of Thomas.

126   The Hawaiians of days past taught that there was a "cave of the beast" within us that was "localized from the stomach down through the sex and evacuation organs" (David Kaonohiokaala Bray, *The Kahuna Religion of Hawaii*, 43).

127   Abuse, physical or sexual, is a behavior of the destructive side of the beast, which in some cases may have been triggered as a result of the person's own experience of being abused as a child.

128 "And God saw that the light was good; and God separated the light from the darkness" Genesis 1:4

129 American Journal of Archaeology, 115, 62.

130 "Jung appeared to be undecided in his own mind about the question of the ontological status of the archetypes (see e.g., 1968d [1936], 58; see also Dourley, 1993); and this state of affairs has led to considerable controversy. But I believe that the ambiguity was necessitated by Jung's inability to scientifically reconcile his conviction that the archetypes are at once embodied structures and bear the imprint of the divine; that is, the archetypes are both structures within the human body, and represent the domain of spirit. Jung's intention was clearly a unitary one, and yet his ontology seemed often to be dualistic, as well as persistently ambiguous, and was necessarily so because the science of his day could not envision a nondualistic conception of spirit and matter.

"Jung's dualism is apparent in his distinction between the archetypes and the instincts which required for him a polarization of the psyche into those products derived from matter and those derived from spirit. He imagined the psyche as the intersection at the apex of two cones, one of spirit and the other of matter (1969a [1946], 215)" (Charles D. Laughlin, http://www.scientificexploration.org/journal/jse_10_3_laughlin.pdf).

131 Diana L. Paxson, *Taking Up the Runes*, 185

132 This is connected with the concept that our conscious mind consistently seeks power. The definition of power is individualistic. In our society, most people equate power with external materialistic things such as status, position, title, money, possessions and even physical attractiveness; consider the amount of cosmetic surgery and the money spent on cosmetics. The majority of these aspects fall within the province of the first chakra.

133 *The Seattle Times*, November 21, 2010, p.A19

134 Reflection of shamanic regeneration.

135 Fideler, *Jesus Christ Sun of God: Ancient Cosmology and Early Christian Symbolism*, 173.

136 Ibid, 173.

137 Cerberus, a ferocious canine with three heads, a lion's claws and Medusa-like mane of snakes, and a venomous serpent for a tail, guarded the entrance to Hades. Herakles manages to subdue Cerberus with his bare hands, puts the demonic dog in chains, and leads him up into the light from the underworld.

138 Tarot card eleven, Power, is connected with the Hebrew letter Kaph. The hieroglyphic meaning of the Kaph is the human hand as the firm grasp. All ideas of power correspond to this letter.

139 This is one of the attributes of a shaman wearing the skin of their totem. Thus, the lion would be considered Herakles' totem or power animal.

140 It is a well-known premise that "power corrupts." However, the power within us is now neutralized instead of being poised to do destructive or abusive things.

Power in its truest sense is neutral. It is the shamans or the wizard's intent that deems power healing or harming. Taming our beast allows us to appropriately use power.

141 John Opsopaus, *Guide to the Pythagorean Tarot* (Llewellyn Publications), 111.

142 Sallie Nichols, *Jung and Tarot*, p. 203

143 Opsopaus, *Guide to the Pythagorean Tarot*, 109.

144 Carol Miller & Guadalupe Rivera, *The Winged Prophet* (Samuel Weiser, Inc., York Beach, Maine, (1994), 143.

145 A term used by psychologists referring to empathy leading to helping activity.

146 Joseph Campbell, *The Power of Myth* (Doubleday, 1988) 22.

147 Broadhurst and Miller, *The Dance of the Dragon*, 168.

148 Hawaiian meaning "foundation for seeking wisdom"

149 Koyasan University, *Mikkyo, Kobo Daishi Kukai and Shingon Buddhism*, 27.

150 *Ibid*, 12.

151 Traditional Sami style of singing.

152 https://eikaivoksille.wordpress.com/

153 Please see the Appendix.

154 The Order and the Doctrine, http://www.sacred-texts.com/cla/pdm/pdm05.htm

155 MJ Harden, *Voices of Wisdom* (Aka Press, Kula, HI, 1999), 34.

156 Husfelt, *Return of a Green Philosophy*, 80 – 81.

157 Edited from Husfelt, *The Return of the Feathered Serpent* (AuthorHouse, 2006), 45.

158 https://www.psychologytoday.com/us/blog/animal-emotions/201801/animal-consciousness-new-report-puts-all-doubts-sleep

159 Ritgerð til M.A., "The Language of Birds in Old Norse Tradition," 3.

160 Harden, *Voices of Wisdom*, 53.

161 Veary, *Change We Must*, 31.

162 Paul Broadhurst, *Tintagel and the Arthurian Mythos* (Pendragon Press, Cornwall, 1992), 84.

163 H. Talat Halman, Ph.D., "The Green Man Symbol of Our Care for Mother Earth," http://www.sevenpillarshouse.org/article/the_green_man/

164 Diane Toomey, "Exploring How and Why Trees 'Talk' to Each Other," Yale Environment 360, September 1, 2016 (https://e360.yale.edu/features/exploring_how_and_why_trees_talk_to_each_other).

165 Winona LaDuk, *All Our Relations*, first published 1999 by South End Press, Cambridge, Massachusetts.

166 Fundamental prayer of the *kahuna*, wise man or shaman.

167   *Lono* was identified with rain and food plants. He was one of the four gods
      (with *Ku*, *Kane*, and his twin

> brother *Kanaloa*) who existed before the world was created. *Lono* was
> also the god of peace. *Lono* is lord of the east and the god of learning. *Lono*
> in Hawaii is associated with cloud signs and the phenomena of storms. . ..
> In prayers to *Lono* the signs of the god are named as thunder, lightning,
> earthquake, the dark cloud, the rainbow, rain, and wind. (Husfelt, *Tequila*
> *and Chocolate*, 492.)

168   Harden, *Voices of Wisdom*, 53.

169   This reference to the eye has an outer and inner combination meaning and
      teaching. On the one hand it refers to our eyes and the focus of our attention
      in life. On the other hand, it refers to our esoteric eye or third eye and its con-
      nection to the pituitary and pineal gland.

170   *Matthew, 6:22-23*

171   Baby eyes are non-judgmental and see life from a non-attached state of being
      where there is never any prejudice but always a sense of openness and new-
      ness. Observing life with the eyes of a baby offers a gift that is always present
      for you. And that gift is beauty. With baby eyes you are seeing from your heart
      all the love and light that is before you without darkness shedding its shadow
      over precious moments of time. A smile and baby eyes may be the means that
      you will need to be able to discover joy and happiness in life.

172   Fideler, *Jesus Christ Sun of God*, 187.

173   http://www.pbs.org/faithandreason/theogloss/logos-body.html

174   Ibid

175   Marcus Tullius Cicero was a Roman statesman, lawyer and Academic Skeptic
      philosopher who wrote extensively on rhetoric, orations, philosophy, and poli-
      tics, and is considered one of Rome's greatest orators and prose stylists.

176   Douglas Gillette, M.A., M.Div., *The Shaman's Secret*, 108.

177   This is a Hawaiian concept that bears some similarity to the Western concept
      of the Holy Grail.

178   Adapted from Husfelt, *Tequila and Chocolate*, 152.

179   Today, one of the most dreaded diseases is cancer. "The body is made up of
      trillions of living cells. Normal body cells grow, divide to make new cells, and
      die in an orderly way. Cancer cell growth is different from normal cell growth.
      Instead of dying, cancer cells continue to grow and form new, abnormal cells"
      (http://www.cancer.org/cancer/cancerbasics/what-is-cancer).

> Philosophically, as well as materialistically, every part of the body dreams—
> including cells. If there has been major wounding from the past, this
> memory is encoded somewhere within the body—within the cells. And
> woundings of the same nature could possibly be in the same set of cells.
> Conducting spiritual, mental, and physical tools of release may possibly
> reprogram the cells and let them die naturally, reflecting the "mental or
> spiritual death" of the wounding and its cellular memory.

180 The throwing of a stone extends as far back as the ancient Greeks where an oath was bonded by "grasping and casting away a stone as an expression of utter irretrievability." (Walter Burkert, *Greek Religion*, 250)

181 Harden, *Voices of Wisdom*, 48 – 49.

182 Veary, *Change We Must*, 36.

183 Adapted from Husfelt, *Tequila and Chocolate*, 7 – 8.

184 Opsopaus, *Guide to the Pythagorean Tarot*, 89.

185 Marios Koutsoukos, *Navel of the Earth* (2016), 71.

186 Paul van Tongeren, "Nietzsche's Greek Measure," Article in The Journal of Nietzsche Studies · January 2002, 5. (https://www.researchgate.net/publication/236803624)

187 Ibid, 14.

188 Passions are all mental functions that disturb the tranquility of the mind.

189 Excerpted from http://www.siue.edu/EASTASIA/paxon_102199.htm

190 John M. Dillon, "Metriopatheia and Apatheia: Some Reflections on a Controversy in Later Greek Ethics," Trinity College Dublin, Ireland, jmdillon@eircom.net.

191 Opsopaus, *Guide to the Pythagorean Tarot*, 89.

192 Nothing in Excess, September 4, 2015, (https://www.intellectualtakeout.org/blog/nothing-excess/)

193 Koutsoukos, *Navel of the Earth*, 62 - 63.

194 The lyre or harp was invented by Mercury, the messenger of the gods, and was owned by Apollo's son, Orpheus. The song of Orpheus and the music of his harp had the power to tame all creatures. He is known as the Bringer of Culture and the Father of Mysticism.

195 Fideler, *The Pythagorean Sourcebook and Library*, 43.

196 Greek pre-Socratic Philosopher

197 Opsopaus, *Guide to the Pythagorean Tarot*, p. 88

198 Edouard Shuré, http://www.sacred-texts.com/cla/pdm/pdm05.htm

199 *Ibid*

200 Hemenway, *Divine Proportion*, 11.

201 Could this be a hint of life everlasting?

202 Nick Anthony Fiorenza, "The Unfoldment of Number," 1995. (https://www.lunarplanner.com/number.html)

203 Hemenway, *Divine Proportion*, 126.

204 Paul van Tongeren, "Nietzsche's Greek Measure," Article in The Journal of Nietzsche Studies · January 2002, 8.

205 Quote of Rev. Dr. JC Husfelt

206 Fideler, The Pythagorean Sourcebook and Library, 34.

207 Concept of the Salish First People of Northwest Coast Canada.

208   Lee and Willis, *Ho'opono*

209   Harden, *Voices of Wisdom*, 109.

210   John D. Pappas, "The Concept of Measure and the Criterion of Sustainability," 81. (http://www.academia.edu/29332856/The_Concept_of_Measure_and_the_Criterion_of_Sustainability_The_St._Johns_Review_)

211   *Atē* was the ancient Greek personified spirit (daimona) of delusion, infatuation, blind folly, rash action and reckless impulse who led men down the path of ruin.

212   Hemenway, *Divine Proportion*, 11 - 12.

213   One of my primary fixed stars, Helical Setting Star is *Sualocin* in the constellation *Delphinus*: the Hebrews knew this constellation as Jonah's big fish. Early Christian interpreters viewed Jonah as a type for Jesus.

214   Rene Guenon, *Fundamental Symbols*, (Quinta Essentia), 110.

215   The tarot is a system of symbolic cards possibly dating from the time of ancient Egypt. The cards are divided into Major and Minor Arcana. The word arcana has the meaning of hidden, secret, or mysterious.

216   Most people know this card as Temperance.

217   Sallie Nichols, *Angels and Mortals*, 198.